ISBN 978-1-331-95330-2
PIBN 10258985

This book is a reproduction of an important historical work. Forgotten Books uses state-of-the-art technology to digitally reconstruct the work, preserving the original format whilst repairing imperfections present in the aged copy. In rare cases, an imperfection in the original, such as a blemish or missing page, may be replicated in our edition. We do, however, repair the vast majority of imperfections successfully; any imperfections that remain are intentionally left to preserve the state of such historical works.

English
Français
Deutsche
Italiano
Español
Português

www.forgottenbooks.com

Mythology Photography **Fiction**
Fishing Christianity **Art** Cooking
Essays Buddhism Freemasonry
Medicine **Biology** Music **Ancient
Egypt** Evolution Carpentry Physics
Dance Geology **Mathematics** Fitness
Shakespeare **Folklore** Yoga Marketing
Confidence Immortality Biographies
Poetry **Psychology** Witchcraft
Electronics Chemistry History **Law**
Accounting **Philosophy** Anthropology
Alchemy Drama Quantum Mechanics
Atheism Sexual Health **Ancient History**
Entrepreneurship Languages Sport
Paleontology Needlework Islam
Metaphysics Investment Archaeology
Parenting Statistics Criminology
Motivational

CHARTER

FOR THE

CITY AND COUNTY

OF

AN FRANCISCO

PREPARED AND PROPOSED BY THE

BOARD OF FREEHOLDERS,

lected November 6, 1894, in pursuance of the provisions
of Section 8, Article XI, of the Constitution
of the State of California.

BOARD OF FREEHOLDERS.

PRESIDENT:
JOSEPH BRITTON.

VICE-PRESIDENT:
GEO. T. MARYE, JR.

JEROME A. ANDERSON,   *STEWART MENZIES,
COLIN M. BOYD,   J. J. O'BRIEN,
HENRY N. CLEMENT,   IRVING M. SCOTT,
WILLIAM F. GIBSON,   LOUIS SLOSS, JR.,
M. H. HECHT,   I. J. TRUMAN,
GUSTAVE H. UMBSEN.

Secretary,   Assistant Secretary,
J. A. VAUGHAN.   T. C. JUDKINS.
                        Clerk,
                        CHAS. A. RITTER.

NOTE.—Fifteen Freeholders were originally elected, but two were declared ineligible by the Supreme Court of California.

*Resigned January 21, 1895.

COMMITTEES.

1. **Boundary, including Rights and Liabilities of the existing Municipality:**
   Messrs. Umbsen, Anderson and Gibson.

2. **The Legislative Department, its Powers and Mode of Procedure:**
   Messrs. Truman, Boyd, *Menzies, Gibson and Clement.

3. **Finance, Revenue and Taxation:**
   Messrs. Boyd, Truman and Marye.

4. **The Executive Department, including the duties of the Municipal Officers thereof:**
   Messrs. *Menzies, Umbsen and Sloss.

5. **The Judicial Department, including the duties of Officers connected with the administration of Law:**
   Messrs. Clement, Gibson and Marye.

6. **Department of Public Works, including Streets, Squares and Parks, and the regulation of Harbor and Wharves:**
   Messrs. Scott, Sloss and *Menzies.

7. **Public Schools and Libraries:**
   Messrs. Gibson, Anderson and O'Brien.

8. **Public Institutions of Charity and Correction:**
   Messrs. Britton, Umbsen and Anderson.

9. **Public Order and Police:**
   Messrs. Marye, Scott and Clement.

10. **The Fire Department:**
    Messrs. Hecht, O'Brien and Scott.

11. **The Health Department:**
    Messrs. Anderson, Boyd and Hecht.

12. **Department of Elections:**
    Messrs. Sloss, Marye and Hecht.

13. **Civil Service:**
    Messrs. O'Brien, Truman and Scott.

14. **Salaries:**
    Messrs. O'Brien, *Menzies and Hecht.

15. **Miscellaneous Provisions and Schedule:**
    Messrs. Gibson, Scott and Boyd.

16. **Revision:**
    Messrs. Clement, Gibson and Marye.

The President, JOSEPH BRITTON, Ex Officio Member of all Committees.

*Resigned January 21, 1895.

CHARTER

Prepared and Proposed for the City and County of
San Francisco

BY THE

BOARD OF FREEHOLDERS

Elected November 6, 1894, in pursuance of the provisions of Section 8, Article XI, of the Constitution of the State of California.

ARTICLE I.

Boundaries, Rights and Liabilities of the Existing Municipality.

SECTION 1. The municipal corporation, now existing, known as the City and County of San Francisco, shall remain and continue a body politic and corporate, in name and in fact, by the name of the City and County of San Francisco, and by that name, shall have perpetual succession, may sue and defend in all Courts and places, and in all matters and proceedings whatever, and may have and use a common seal, and the same alter at pleasure, and may purchase, receive, hold and enjoy real and personal property within and without the City and County of San Francisco, and sell, convey, mortgage and dispose of the same for the common benefit; receive bequests, gifts and donations of all kinds of property within and without the city and county, in fee simple, or in trust for charitable or other purposes, and do all acts necessary to carry out the purposes of such gifts, bequests and donations, with power to manage, sell, lease, or otherwise dispose of the same in accordance with the terms of the gift, bequest or trust.

SEC. 2. The boundaries of the City and County of San Francisco shall be as follows:

Beginning at the southwest corner of the City and County of San Francisco, being the northwest corner of San Mateo county in the Pacific Ocean, and on the line of the western boundary of the State of California three miles from shore, and also on the extension of the northern line of Township Three South, Mount Diablo Base and Meridian; thence northerly along the western boundary of the State of California to the southwest corner of Marin county as now established by section 3957 of the Political Code; thence easterly to the western extension of low water line on the northern side of the entrance to San Francisco Bay, and on the south line of Marin county; thence easterly through Point Bonita and Point Caballo (or Cavallo), to the most southeastern point of Angel .Island, all on the southern line of Marin county, as now established in said section 3957 of the Political Code; thence northerly along the easterly line of Marin county to the northwest point of Golden Rock (also known as Red Rock), being a common corner of Marin, Contra Costa and San Francisco counties; thence due southeast four and one-half miles, more or less, to a point distant three statute miles from the natural high water mark on the eastern shore of San Francisco Bay, being a common corner of Contra Costa, Alameda and San Francisco counties; thence southerly and southeasterly and along the western boundary of Alameda county as now established by section 3953 of the Political Code, to a point on the extension of the northern line of Township Three South, Mount Diablo Base and Meridian (considered as extending across said Bay); thence west along the last named line to the place of beginning.

The Islands in said Bay, known as Alcatraces, Yerba Buena and Mission Rock, and the Islands in said Ocean' known as Farallones, shall be a part of said city and county.

SEC. 3. The public buildings, lands and property, all rights of property and rights of action, all moneys, revenues, and income belonging or appertaining to the City and County of San Francisco, are hereby declared to be vested in the said City and County of San Francisco.

SEC. 4. The said City and County of San Francisco shall continue to have, hold and enjoy all public buildings, lands, wharves, waters, property real and personal, rights of property, rights of action, suits, actions, moneys, revenue, income, books, documents, records, archives, claims, demands, and things in possession and action of every nature and description, and shall be subject to all the obligations, debts, liabilities, dues and duties of the existing municipality,

SEC. 5. Suits, actions and proceedings may be brought in the name of said city and county, for the recovery of any property, money or thing belonging thereto, in law or equity, or dedicated to public use therein, or for the enforcement of any rights of, or contracts with, said city and county, whether made or arising or accruing before or after the adoption of this Charter; and all existing suits, actions and proceedings in the courts or elsewhere, to which said city and county is a party, shall continue to be carried on by or against said city and county.

SEC. 6. No recourse shall be had against said City and County for damage to person or property suffered or sustained by, or because of, the defective condition of any street or public highway of said city and county, or in consequence of any such street or public highway being out of repair or in condition to endanger persons or property passing thereon; but if such defect in the street or public highway shall have existed for the period of twenty-four hours or more after notice thereof to the Mayor of said city and county, then the person or persons on whom the law may have imposed the obligation to repair such defect in the street or public highway, and also the officer or officers through whose official negligence such defect remains unrepaired, shall be jointly and severally liable to the party injured for the damage sustained.

ARTICLE II.

Legislative Department.

CHAPTER I.

OF THE SUPERVISORS.

SECTION 1. The Legislative power of the City and County of San Francisco shall be vested in a legislative body which shall be designated the Board of Supervisors; such body is also designated in this Charter the Supervisors.

Sec. 2. The Board of Supervisors shall consist of twelve members, who shall be elected by general ticket from the city and county at large, and shall hold office for two years.

Sec. 3. No person shall be eligible to the office of member of the Board of Supervisors unless he shall have been for at least five years continuously a qualified elector of said city and county; and no person shall be eligible to act as such member who shall have been convicted of any infamous crime, or who shall have been removed from any municipal office by the Mayor, the Board of Supervisors, or the judgment of a court; and any such conviction during his term of office shall cause the forfeiture of his seat in said Board.

Sec. 4. Seven members of the Board shall constitute a quorum, but a less number may adjourn from day to day and compel the attendance of absent members in such manner and under such penalties as the Board may prescribe.

Sec. 5. The Board shall:

1. Appoint a Clerk, Sergeant-at-Arms, and when authorized to do so by ordinance, such additional clerks and other assistants as may be deemed necessary.

2. Establish rules for its proceedings.

3. Keep a journal of its proceedings and allow the same to be published. The ayes and noes on any question shall, on demand of any member, be taken and entered therein.

4. Have authority to punish its members for disorderly or contemptuous behavior in its presence, and to expel any member by the affirmative vote of not less than nine members, specifying in the order of expulsion the cause thereof.

5. Have power to compel the attendance of witnesses and production of papers pertinent to any business before such Board.

Sec. 6. The Mayor shall be the presiding officer of the Board of Supervisors. In the absence of the Mayor the Board may appoint a presiding officer *pro tempore* from its own members, who shall, however, have the same right to vote as other members.

Sec. 7. The Board shall meet upon the first Monday of each month, or, if that day be a legal holiday, then upon the next day, and the Board shall not adjourn for more than seven days, or to any other place than its regular place of meeting. The meetings of the Board shall be public.

SEC. 8. The Clerk of the Board of Supervisors may administer oaths and affirmations in all matters pertaining to the affairs of his office without charge, and shall perform such services as may be prescribed by said Board. He shall have the custody of the seal of said city and county, and of all leases, grants and other documents, records and papers. His signature shall be necessary to all leases, grants and conveyances, and he shall have the custody of all resolutions and ordinances of said city and county.

SEC. 9. No Supervisor shall hold any other office, Federal, State or Municipal, or be an employee of said city and county, or be directly or indirectly interested in any contract with said city and county, or with or for any Department or Institution thereof; or advance money or furnish material or supplies for the performance of any such contract; or furnish or become surety for the performance of any such contract; or directly or indirectly recommend, solicit, advise, request, or in any manner use his influence to obtain the appointment of any person to any office, position, place or employment under the city and county Government, or under any Department, Board or officer thereof; but nothing in this section shall impair the right of a Supervisor to nominate and recommend any person for any office or position to be filled by appointment or election by the Supervisors of which he is a member. Upon taking office, each Supervisor shall make and file in the office of the Clerk of the Supervisors an affidavit that he will faithfully comply with and abide by all the requirements of this section. A violation of any of the provisions of this section shall cause a forfeiture of his office, and render him ineligible to any office in the future.

SEC. 10. Every Legislative Act of said city and county shall be by ordinance. The enacting clause of every ordinance shall be: "*Be it ordained by the Board of Supervisors of the City and County of San Francisco, as follows:*" No ordinance shall be passed except by bill, and no bill shall be so amended as to change its original purpose.

SEC. 11. No bill shall become an ordinance unless on its final passage at least seven members of the Board vote in its favor, and the vote be taken by ayes and noes, and the names of the members voting for and against the same be entered in the Journals.

SEC. 12. No ordinance shall be revised, re-enacted or amended by reference to its title; but the ordinance to be revised or re-enacted, or the section thereof amended, shall be re-enacted at length as revised or amended.

SEC. 13. Every ordinance shall embrace but one subject, which subject shall be expressed in its title; if any subject be embraced in an ordinance and not expressed in its title, such ordinance shall be void only as to so much thereof as is not expressed in its title.

SEC. 14. When a bill is put upon its final passage in the Board and fails to pass, and a motion is made to reconsider, the vote upon such motion shall not be acted on before the next meeting of said Board. No bill for the grant of any franchise shall be put upon its final passage within ninety days after its introduction. Every ordinance shall, after amendment, be laid over for one week before its final passage.

SEC. 15. No ordinance shall take effect until ten days after its passage unless otherwise expressed in said ordinance.

SEC. 16. Every bill which shall have passed the Board, and which shall have been duly authenticated, shall be presented to the Mayor for his approval. The Mayor shall return such bill to the Board within ten days after receiving it. If he approve it he shall sign it, and it shall then become an ordinance. If he disapprove it he shall specify his objections thereto in writing. If he do not return it with such disapproval within the time above specified, it shall take effect as if he had approved it. The objections of the Mayor shall be entered at large on the Journal of the Board, and the Board shall cause the same to be immediately published. The Board shall, after five and within thirty days after such bill shall have been so returned, reconsider and vote upon the same; and if the same shall, upon reconsideration, be again passed by the affirmative vote of not less than nine members, the presiding officer shall certify that fact on the bill, and when so certified, the bill shall become an ordinance with like effect as if it had received the approval of the Mayor; but if the bill shall fail to receive upon the first vote thereon nine affirmative votes it shall be deemed finally lost. The vote on such reconsideration shall be taken by ayes and noes, and the names of the members voting for or against the same shall be entered in the Journal.

SEC. 17. All ordinances and resolutions shall be deposited with the Clerk of the Board, who shall record the same at length in a suitable book.

SEC. 18. No ordinance making a general appropriation shall be passed, but every appropriation shall be for the specific amount of the demand to be paid; and each ordinance authorizing the payment of money shall contain one demand only, which shall be expressed in its title.

SEC. 19. Every ordinance or resolution providing for any specific improvement, the granting of any privilege, or involving the lease, appropriation or disposition of public property, or the expenditure of public money (except sums less than five hundred dollars), or levying any tax or assessment, and every ordinance providing for the imposition of a new duty or penalty, shall, after its introduction, be published, with the ayes and noes, at least five successive days before final action upon the same; and if such bill be amended, the bill as amended shall be published for a like period before final action thereon. *Provided*, that the provisions of this section shall not authorize the Supervisors to pass any ordinance or resolution for the appropriation or expenditure of public moneys amounting to five hundred dollars or less, unless the same be passed by a majority vote of said Board upon a call of yeas and nays. *Provided*, further, that in cases of great necessity the officers and heads of the departments may, with the consent of the Mayor, expend such sums of money not to exceed $50 as shall be necessary to meet the requirements of such emergency.

CHAPTER II.

OF THE POWERS OF THE SUPERVISORS.

SECTION 1. Subject to the provisions, limitations and restrictions in this Charter contained, the Supervisors shall have power to pass ordinances:

1. To make and enforce within the limits of said city and county all such local, police, sanitary and other laws and regulations as are not in conflict with general laws or this Charter.

2. To regulate and control the use of the streets, sidewalks, highways, roads and public places for any and all purposes; to prevent encroachments upon and obstruction to the same, and require the removal of any encroachment or obstruction thereon.

3. To regulate and control the use of the streets and sidewalks for signs, sign posts, awnings, awning posts, drinking fountains, horse troughs, urinals, telegraph posts; for traffic and sales therein; for exhibiting banners, placards or flags in or across the same, or from houses or other buildings, and for all other purposes.

4. To regulate the cleaning of the streets, sidewalks and gutters, and prevent the depositing of ashes, offal, dirt, rubbish or garbage in the same.

5. To regulate the opening of street surfaces for the laying of gas or water mains, or telegraph or telephone wires; for the bnilding and repair of sewers; for the erecting of gas or electric lights, or for any other use or purpose.

6. To regulate the numbering of houses and lots and the naming of streets, public places and thoroughfares.

7. In relation to street beggars, vagrants and mendicants, and the exhibition and distribution of advertisements or handbills along the streets or in public places.

8. In relation to intoxication, fighting, quarreling and vulgar language in the streets and other public places, and in relation to carrying concealed weapons.

9. In relation to the construction, maintenance, repair and removal of public fountains for the use of persons and animals on the streets and in other public places.

10. To regulate and to provide for the safety and comfort of people attending places of public amusements and regulate or prohibit public processions.

11. To restrain and prevent any riot, mob, noise, disturbance, or disorderly assembly or amusement dangerous to persons or property in any street, house or place.

12. To permit the laying down of railroad tracks and running cars thereon, along any street or portion of a street, for the sole purpose of excavating and filling in a street or portion of a street or the adjoining land, for such limited time as may be necessary for such purpose and no longer.

13. To provide for lighting the streets, squares, parks and public places, buildings and offices; and for enclosing, improving and regulating public grounds.

14. To fix the limits within which wooden buildings or structures shall not be erected, placed or maintained, and to prohibit the same within such limits.

15. To prohibit, suppress, regulate or exclude from certain limits all houses of ill-fame, prostitution and gaming; to prohibit, suppress or exclude from certain limits all occupations, houses, places, pastimes, amusements, exhibitions and practices which are against good morals and contrary to public order and decency, or dangerous to the public safety.

16. To regulate the manufacture, transportation, sale, disposition, storage and use of firearms, firecrackers, fireworks and all explosive or combustible materials and substances; the manufacture of acids, and the maintenance of acid works, slaughter houses, brick kilns, tanneries, laundries, foundries, steam boilers, and factories using steam boilers, and all other manufactories, works and occupations of every description that may affect the public safety, health or comfort, and to exclude them from certain limits.

17. To protect the health, comfort and security of the inhabitants, and the safety and security of property and life; to exclude from certain limits, hospitals, institutions and places for the treatment of disease, or for the care of sick or insane persons; to regulate all noxious trades, and restrict the prosecution thereof to such limits as may from time to time seem proper, or exclude them from said city and county; to make regulations for protection against fire, and to make such rules and regulations concerning the construction and use of buildings as may be necessary for the safety of the inhabitants; to provide for the examination, approval or disapproval of the plans and specifications of all buildings about to be constructed, and to prevent the construction thereof contrary to the provisions of any ordinance; to provide

for the examination of all buildings and the removal thereof if found unsafe or constructed contrary to ordinance.

18. To authorize the establishment and maintenance of crematories and cemeteries, to regulate the same, and exclude them from certain limits.

19. To provide for the abatement or summary removal of any nuisance.

20. To regulate hackney carriages and public passenger vehicles, and fix the rates to be charged for the transportation of persons or personal baggage; to regulate all vehicles used for the conveyance of merchandise, earth or ballast; to exclude certain classes of vehicles from the use of certain streets; to prescribe the width of the tires of all vehicles, and the weight to be carried by said vehicles; and to regulate drivers, carriers, runners and solicitors.

21. In relation to the construction, repair, care and use of markets and market places, and of places of public amusement and public assemblage.

22. In relation to the construction, repair and use of vaults, cisterns, areas, hydrants, pumps and sewers.

23. To provide a public pound and a pound keeper, with necessary assistants, and to fix the salary of the pound keeper and his assistants, which shall be paid only out of fines collected and paid into the Treasury for the redemption of impounded animals; to prescribe fines for the redemption of animals duly impounded, and to provide for the collection of such fines and their payment into the Treasury on the day they are received; to prevent animals from running at large, and to provide for impounding or killing them when found running at large; to provide for the removal and disposition of animals or vehicles found unattended in any street or public place.

Sec. 24. To provide for suitable buildings, rooms or accommodations for all Courts, Departments, Boards and Officers, together with all necessary attendants, furniture, fuel, lights and stationery for the convenient transaction of business.

25. To provide and maintain a morgue.

26. To provide for places for the detention of witnesses separate and apart from places where criminals, or persons accused of public offenses are imprisoned.

27. To regulate and provide for the employment on the public works of said city and county of prisoners sentenced to labor thereon, and to make regulations requiring prisoners not sentenced to imprisonment in the State Prison, to be sentenced to such labor either in the chain-gang or elsewhere, as the Supervisors may deem expedient; to establish, maintain and regulate, and change, discontinue and re-establish city and county jails, prisons, and houses of correction and other places of detention, punishment, confinement and reformation, and to establish in connection therewith, manufacturing or laboring establishments.

28. To purchase or acquire by condemnation such property as may be needed for public use.

29. To provide water for municipal purposes.

30. To regulate the quality, capacity and location of water and gas pipes, mains and fire plugs, and to provide for and regulate the construction and repair of hydrants, fire plugs, cisterns and pumps, and such other appliances as may be used in the distribution of water or gas in the streets, public places and public buildings.

31. To fix and determine by ordinance in the month of February of each year, to take effect on the first day of July thereafter, the rates or compensation to be collected by any person, company or corporation in the city and county, for the use of water, and gas or other illuminating power, supplied to the city and county or the inhabitants thereof, and to prescribe the quality of gas or other illuminating power.

32. To regulate and impose a license tax upon public amusements, shows and exhibitions, pawnbrokers and railroad passenger cars; upon the manufacture, sale, transportation or storage of any combustibles or explosives; upon astrologers and fortune tellers, who practice their profession for hire; upon billiard tables, bowling alleys, shooting galleries, and other games and amusements kept or conducted for gain or hire; upon the sale at retail of tobacco, cigars, cigarettes, alcoholic and malt liquors; and upon all such other callings, trades, employments, business and places, not prohibited by law, that may require special police surveillance, or that may be prejudicial to public morals and the general welfare.

33. To impose a license tax on dogs.

2

34. To provide for the collection of licenses and municipal revenues and fix the amount thereof.

35. To prescribe fines, forfeitures and penalties for the breach of any ordinance and for a violation of any provision of this Charter; but no penalty shall exceed the amount of five hundred dollars or six months' imprisonment, or both.

36. To provide for the security, custody and administration of all property of said city and county.

37. To make rules and regulations for the government of all servants, employees, officers and departments, and to fix the fees and charges for all official services, and to fix salaries and wages that are not fixed by general laws or this Charter.

38. To allow and order paid out of the various Funds provided in this Charter, the sums respectively chargeable thereto.

39. To allow and order paid out of the proper fund such sums, not to exceed five thousand dollars in any one fiscal year, as may be deemed necessary for the employment of special counsel.

40. To allow and order paid out of the proper fund such sums as may be necessary for burying the indigent dead.

41. To appropriate out of the proper fund a sum not exceeding two hundred and fifty dollars each month for the enforcement of the law in relation to cruelty to children, and to authorize and regulate the payment of the same, or some part thereof, to any Society that shall most efficiently aid in the enforcement of such law.

42. To appropriate out of the proper fund a sum not exceeding five hundred dollars each month, for the care and cure of confirmed inebriates, and the temporary detention of the insane or such persons as may be charged with insanity pending examination.

43. To appropriate out of the proper fund such sums as may be paid into the Treasury from fines collected on conviction of persons charged with cruelty to animals, and to authorize and regulate the payment of the same or some part thereof to any society that shall efficiently aid in such convictions.

44. Until the completion of the New City Hall, to provide in the annual tax levy for a tax upon the real and personal property in said city and county, at the

rate of ten cents on the one hundred dollars for the completion of said New City Hall; and to appropriate the money so raised to its completion.

45. To provide for the payment of a proper compensation to those appointed by the Superior Court, to report the testimony in cases to which the people or said city and county may be a party.

46. To provide for the payment of compensation to such interpreters, not exceeding five, as may be appointed by the Judges of the Superior Court, to interpret testimony in criminal causes in said Court or the Police Court, or upon inquests and examinations. Such compensation shall not exceed one hundred dollars a month for each interpreter.

47. To offer rewards not exceeding five hundred dollars, at any one time, for the apprehension and conviction of any person who may have committed a felony in said city and county, and to authorize the payment thereof out of the proper fund.

48. To provide in the annual tax levy for a special fund to be used in the construction of a general system of drainage for said city and county.

49. To provide a common seal for said city and county, and from time to time to alter and change the same; and also to provide for seals for the several Departments, Boards and Officers of said city and county, and for the Police Court, and for altering and changing the same.

50. To fix the hours of labor or service required of all laborers in the service of the city and county, and to fix their compensation.

51. To open, close, straighten, or widen any street, road or highway; to open and lay out any new street or highway through public or private property, upon making compensation to all persons whose property may be taken therefor or injuriously affected thereby, upon the conditions and in the manner by law and in this Charter provided; and in like manner to change the grade of any street, road or highway. No change of grade shall be made without providing compensation in such manner as may be provided by law and ordinance, to persons whose property may be injuriously affected by such proposed change of grade; but no compensation shall be allowed for damage to gas or water pipes, rail-

way tracks, telegraph posts or wires, or other property or thing laid above, along, in, or under any street, highway, park, place, or other public property.

52. To permit tunnels, in accordance with such rules and regulations as the Supervisors may prescribe, to be constructed and maintained under the surface of any street, road, highway, public park, square, or place, through lands belonging to said city and county, for the passage of pedestrians or railroad cars propelled by steam or other motive power, and other carriages and vehicles for the conveyance of merchandise and passengers. No such permission shall be granted without the written consent of persons owning two-thirds of the frontage of the property upon the line of that portion of the street under which such tunnel is to be run, under the direction of the Board of Public Works, and compensation shall be made, in such manner as may be provided by law and ordinance, to persons whose property may be injuriously affected by any such tunnel.

53. To regulate all street railroads, tracks and cars, and, when and where necessary, to compel the owners of two or more of such roads using the same street for any distance, to use the same tracks and to equitably divide the expense thereof between the owners; to fix and establish and reduce the fares and charges for transporting passengers and goods thereon; to regulate rates of speed, and pass ordinances to protect the public from danger or inconvenience in the operation of such roads; to compel the owners of street railroads to pave and keep in repair the street between their rails, and also between their tracks, and for at least two feet on the outside of the same, including all switches, turnouts and side tracks.

54. To grant authority, for a term not exceeding forty years, to construct street railways and lay down street railroad tracks upon or over any of the streets of said city and county except streets, or parts of streets, reserved for boulevards or carriage driveways, upon which cars may be propelled by horses, mules, steam, or other motive power, or by wire ropes running under the streets and moved by stationary engines, upon such terms and under such restrictions, limitations and conditions as may be required by law and provided by ordinance, and to regulate the rates of fare to be

charged by any person, company or corporation to which such authority may be granted.

55. To allow all trans-continental, or other steam railroad companies or corporations, having not less than fifty miles of road actually constructed and in operation, and having reached the city and county line, to enter said city and county and make its way to the water front at the most convenient point for public convenience; but no exclusive right, franchise or privilege shall be granted to such railroad company; and the use of all such rights, privileges and franchises shall at all times be subject to regulation by the Supervisors. Every ordinance granting such right, privilege or franchise, shall be upon the conditions that said company or corporation shall pave and keep in repair the street from curb to curb, and that said company or corporation shall allow any railroad company or corporation to which a similar right, privilege or franchise may be granted, to use in common with it the same track or tracks upon such terms as the Supervisors shall determine.

56. To make appropriations allowed by law or this Charter.

57. For the conveyance of lands in accordance with the provisions of the Act of the Legislature of the State of California, entitled, ''An Act to expedite the settlement of land titles in the City and County of San Francisco, and to ratify and confirm the acts and proceedings of certain of the authorities thereof,'' approved March 24, 1870.

58. To provide for the execution of all trusts confided to said city and county.

59. To transfer from one department of the city government vacant and unused lots to another department, if the same are needed by such other department. Each department shall be correspondingly credited and debited for the amount of the assessable value of the property thus transferred.

60. To provide for the sale or lease of all lands now or hereafter owned by said city and county, not dedicated or reserved for public use; but all leases and sales shall be made at public auction after publication of notice thereof for at least three weeks. No sale shall be authorized, except by ordinance passed by the affirma-

tive vote of all the members of said Board, or any lease made for a longer period than two years except by an affirmative vote passed by not less than nine members.

61. To provide for the sale at public auction, after advertising for five days, of all personal property unfit or unnecessary for the use of said city and county.

62. To provide for the purchase of property levied upon or under execution in favor of said city and county; but the amount bid on such purchase shall not exceed the amount of the judgment and costs.

63. To incur an indebtedness exceeding the revenue for any fiscal year in case of great public calamity or danger, such as earthquakes, conflagrations, pestilence, invasion or other great and unforeseen emergency. The ordinance for such purpose must be passed by the affirmative vote of not less than nine members of the Board, and be approved by the Mayor. Before or at the time of incurring such indebtedness provision shall be made for the collection of an annual tax sufficient to pay the interest on such indebtedness as it falls due, and also to constitute a Sinking Fund for the payment of the principal thereof, within twenty years from the time of contracting the same. No such indebtedness shall be incurred without the assent of two-thirds of the qualified electors of said city and county voting at an election held for that purpose.

64. To enter into negotiations at as early a date as they may deem for the best interests of the city and county and the inhabitants thereof, for the permanent acquisition, either by purchase or by construction, by said city and county of Water Works, Gas Works, Electric Light Works, Steam, Water or Electric Power Works, Telephone Lines and Street Railroads, and to submit to the qualified electors of said city and county such proposition or propositions. *Provided*, that in making such negotiations they shall take into account the acquisition of existing plants in case the same are desirable and can be acquired upon terms as reasonable as such Works could be procured by construction; *provided*, further, that all estimates of the cost and value of such Works shall be first made and recommended to be reasonable by the Board of Public Works before submission to the citizens; and, *provided* further, that the said submission to the electors of all such proposition or

propositions shall be made in accordance with the provisions of Article XIV, Section 16, of this Charter.

65. Should the electors at any such city election decide to purchase all or any of said properties, it shall be the duty of the Supervisors to open prompt negotiations for the purchase of the same, and if such negotiations, after a reasonable interval, not in any case to exceed six months, shall fail, the Supervisors shall cause to be instituted proper legal proceedings, under the right of Eminent Domain, or otherwise, to condemn and acquire such property or properties.

66. The Board of Supervisors of the City and County of San Francisco within thirty days after this Charter shall have taken effect, shall by ordinance prescribe the number and the salaries of all officers and employees of said city and county not elsewhere provided for in this Charter; and shall in the month of July of each year, by ordinance, fix and establish, and may reduce, but shall not increase the salaries and wages of all such officers, deputies, clerks and employees of said city and county, whose salaries shall have been fixed by them. *Provided*, that the Supervisors are prohibited from reducing the salaries of officers, clerks or employees to a nominal sum, for the purpose of causing such officers, clerks or employees to resign or withdraw from their positions; and *provided further*, that nothing in this section or elsewhere in this Charter shall be so construed as to prevent the grading of the salaries of officers, clerks and employees under civil service rules so that the same may be gradually increased by efficient and long continued faithful service.

SEC. 2. Every ordinance creating or providing for the employment of any deputy, clerk or employee under said city and county, or any Department, Board or officer thereof, other than those specifically named and provided for in this| Charter, shall expire by limitation at the end of one year from its passage; but nothing herein contained shall prevent the re-enactment thereof in the same manner and for the same period that the original ordinance was passed; and no salary or compensation shall be drawn or allowed for any interval of time after such termination and before such re-enactment; but nothing in this section shall be so construed as to impair or effect in any way the provisions of Article XII of this Charter relating to the Civil Service.

Sec. 3. The Supervisors shall constitute the Board of Equalization of said city and county, and shall meet at the time, have the powers, and perform the duties concerning the equalization of taxes prescribed by the general revenue laws of this State. The President *pro tempore* of the Board shall be the presiding officer of the Board of Equalization, and the Clerk of the Board shall be ex officio Clerk thereof.

Sec. 4. The Supervisors shall have power to pass all ordinances and laws and make such rules and regulations as shall be necessary to carry into execution the powers vested by this Charter or by law in said city and county, or in any Department or Officer thereof.

Sec. 5. The Board shall have power to appoint from its members a Committee consisting of three, to be denominated " Finance Committee," and to fill all vacancies in said Committee. Said Committee shall have power to investigate the transactions and accounts of all officers having the collection, custody or disbursement of public money, or having the power to approve, allow or audit demands on the Treasury; shall have free access to any records, books and papers in all public offices; shall have power to administer oaths and affirmations, and to examine witnesses, and compel their attendance before them by subpœna. Said Committee may visit any of the public offices when and as often as they think proper, and make their examinations and investigations therein, without hindrance. It shall be the duty of said Committee as often as once in every six months, to examine the official bonds of all city and county officers, and inquire into and investigate the sufficiency and solvency of the sureties thereon, and report the facts to the Mayor. Such report shall specify each bond with the sureties and the amounts for which each surety is bound, and state whether or not they are deemed sufficient and solvent. Upon such report the Mayor shall act so as to protect the city, and may require new bonds when necessary, and he may suspend the officer till a sufficient bond is filed and approved. In the exercise of its functions, the concurrence of two members of the Committee shall be deemed sufficient. The Committee shall keep a record of its proceedings, with the names of the witnesses examined and a substantial statement of the evidence taken. If from the examination made by the Committee it shall appear that a misdemeanor in office, or a defalcation, has been committed by any officer, said Committee shall immediately report to the Mayor, who, if he approve said report, shall forthwith suspend such officer and take proceedings against him before the Board of Supervisors. Any police officer shall execute the process and orders of said Committee.

.. Sec. 6. The Supervisors shall grant no franchise, right or privilege except upon the conditions that the grantee thereof shall within six months thereafter commence the exercise and enjoyment of the same, and upon proof to the satisfaction of said Board that the franchise, right or privilege shall have been in disuse, in whole or in part, for the period of six months, said Board by resolution shall declare the same forfeited to the extent of such disuse.

Sec. 7. No exclusive franchise or privilege shall be granted for laying pipes or other conduits under any of the public streets or through any public place for the use of any telegraph, telephone or other mode of transmitting intelligence, or for the transmission of steam, electric or other motive power, or for the conveyance of water or illuminating gas.

Sec. 8. The Supervisors shall grant no franchise to construct a street railway or lay down street railroad tracks upon or over any of the streets of said city and county, except in the manner and on the terms following, viz.:

Upon application being made to the Supervisors for such franchise to construct and operate a street railway along and upon any of said streets the Supervisors shall, by resolution, determine whether such franchise, or any part thereof should be granted; and after such determination, it shall cause notice of such application and resolution to be published for ten days (legal holidays excepted), and shall, in said notice, specify the route over and along which it has determined to grant said franchise; and shall offer to grant the same to the person, company or corporation who will pay the highest sum for the franchise, and who will, in addition, agree that, beginning one year after said railway shall have commenced operation, the holder of said franchise will pay into the City and County Treasury, within ten days after the close of each and every month thereafter, not less than two per centum upon the gross receipts of such railway during that month.

Bidding for such franchises must be in accordance with the provisions of this Charter in relation to bids made to the Board of Public Works, so far as such provisions may be applicable, and the Supervisors may reject any and all bids, and may refuse to grant a franchise for any part of the route for which application was made.

If any bid be accepted, the franchise must be granted upon the express condition, in addition to the conditions required by law, and in addition to such other conditions as may be prescribed by the Supervisors, that said per centum of the gross receipts of said railway shall be paid into the Treasury on or before the tenth day of the next ensuing month after such gross receipts shall have been earned; and upon the further condition that the whole of said railway shall be continuously operated, and that, at the end of said term the road-track and bed of such railway shall become the property of said city and county; and that the grantees will, within one hundred days after the date of said grant commence the construction of such railway, and continuously thereafter, in each and every month until the completion thereof, expend in such construction at least the sum of three thousand dollars. The failure, in any one month, to comply with the last specified condition shall work an immediate forfeiture of said franchise and the road or track theretofore constructed thereunder. There shall be no power in the Supervisors to relieve from said forfeiture or from any of said conditions.

No street railway franchise heretofore or hereafter granted shall be continued, extended or renewed except upon the terms and in the manner herein prescribed.

All moneys received for such franchises and in payment of the said per centum shall be credited to the proper fund.

Sec. 9. The Supervisors shall not authorize the placing or continuing of any obstruction upon any street or sidewalk, except during the construction or repair of a building on a lot abutting on the same.

Sec. 10. The Supervisors shall make no appropriation in aid of any corporation, person or society, unless expressly authorized by this Charter.

SEC. 11. All claims for damages against the city and county must be presented to the Board of Supervisors and filed with the Clerk within six months after the occurrence from which the damages arose.

SEC. 12. The Supervisors may, by ordinance, establish Police Courts.

SEC. 13. It shall not be lawful for the Supervisors, or for any Board, Department, officer or authority having power to incur, authorize or contract liabilities against the Treasury of said city and county, to incur, authorize, allow, contract for, pay or render payable in the present or future, in any one month, any expenditure, demand or demands against said Treasury, or any of the Specific Funds thereof, which, taken with all other expenditures, indebtedness or liability made or incurred up to the time in such month of making or incurring the same, shall exceed one-twelfth part of the amount of money provided by the Supervisors and actually collected and paid into the Specific Fund, as and for the income and revenue of the fiscal year during which such liability, expenditure or demand is incurred, and apportioned to the Specific Fund to be charged therewith, and allowed, by law in force at the time such expenditure is made or liability incurred, to be expended out of such Specific Fund as the money apportioned to same for such fiscal year. If, at the beginning of any month, any money remains unexpended in any of the Specific Funds set apart for maintaining the municipal government, and which might lawfully have been expended the preceding month, such unexpended sum or sums, except so much thereof as may be requisite to pay all unpaid claims upon such Specific Fund, that have been duly audited, may be carried forward in the same Specific Fund and expended by order of the Supervisors in any succeeding month of such fiscal year but not afterwards, except in payment of claims lawfully incurred during such fiscal year; but the sums so carried forward in the Common School Fund shall be expended by order of the Board of Education.

1. In case of any great public calamity or danger, such as earthquakes, conflagration, pestilence, invasion, insurrection or other unforseen emergency, the provis-

ions of this section may be temporarily suspended as to any lawful contract, authorization or expenditure necessary to avert, mitigate or relieve the evil; *provided*, that such expenditure, contract or authorization shall be passed by the unanimous vote of the Board of Supervisors and entered in the journal and approved by the Mayor, Auditor and Treasurer, and the character and fact of such emergency must be recited in the ordinance authorizing such action.

2. All contracts, authorizations, allowances, payments, and liability to pay, made or attempted to be made in violation of the provisions of this section, shall be absolutely void, and shall never be the foundation or basis of a claim against the Treasury; and all officers are charged with notice of the condition of the Treasury, and of the extent of the demands against the same, and any officer violating the provisions of this Section shall be personally liable for any liability so incurred.

SEC. 14. No expenditure, debt or liability shall be made, contracted or incurred during any fiscal year that cannot be paid out of the revenues provided for such fiscal year. The city and county shall not, nor shall the Supervisors, the Board of Education, or any Board, Department or officer incur any indebtedness or liability in any manner, or for any purpose, exceeding in any year the income and revenue provided for it for such fiscal year. All contracts, indebtedness or liabilities incurred contrary to the provisions of this section shall be void, and shall not be paid out of the Treasury or constitute or be the foundation of any claim, demand or liability, legal or equitable, against said city and county. The words expenditure, indebtedness and liability herein used shall include official salaries and the pay of all employees of said city and county, or of any of its departments.

SEC. 15. No part of the income or revenue provided for any particular fiscal year shall be applied in payment of any indebtedness or liability incurred during any previous fiscal year, the Sinking Funds and the interest upon the Funded debt alone excepted.

SEC. 16. Except as otherwise expressly authorized in this Charter, the Supervisors, Board of Education or any other Board, Department or officer shall not give one demand preference over another in the authorization, allowance or approval thereof; but demands shall be acted upon in the order in which they are presented.

SEC. 17. All ordinances or resolutions appropriating money or for the incurring of indebtedness or liability against the Treasury, introduced in the Board of Supervisors, or in the Board of Education, or other Department or authority, must, before being passed, be presented to the Auditor, and until he certifies in writing upon such ordinance or resolution that such appropriation can be made or indebtedness incurred without violating any of the provisions of this Charter, no further action shall be had upon the same. Such certificate shall not take the place of the allowance of such demand and final action of the Auditor thereon.

SEC. 18. Neither the Supervisors, nor any officer, Board, Department, or authority, shall allow, make valid, or in any manner recognize any demand against the city and county, which was not at the time of its creation a valid claim against the same, nor shall they, or any of them, ever allow or authorize to be paid, any demand which, without such action, would be invalid, or which shall then be barred by any statute of limitation, or for which said city and county was never liable.

CHAPTER III.

OF CONTRACTS.

SECTION 1. All contracts for an amount exceeding five hundred dollars, for goods, merchandise, stores, supplies, subsistence, printing, or other work or thing for said city and county, as well as for all subsistence, supplies, drugs, and other necessary articles and things for hospitals, prisons, public institutions and other departments not otherwise specifically provided for in this Charter, must be made by the Supervisors with the lowest bidder offering adequate security, after due public notice published for not less than ten days; and no purchase thereof or liability therefor shall be made or created except by contract. Where the amount of the bid shall exceed five thousand dollars, all proposals shall be accompanied with a certificate of deposit or certified check on a solvent bank or banking house in said city and county, for one thousand dollars, and where it shall be less than five thousand dollars, of ten per centum on the amount of the bid, payable at sight to the order of the Clerk of the Supervisors. If the bidder to whom the contract is awarded shall for five days after such award fail or neglect to enter into the contract and file the required bond, the Clerk shall draw the money due on said certificate of deposit or check, and pay the same into the Treasury; and under no circumstances shall the certificate of deposit or check or the proceeds thereof be returned to such defaulting bidder. All such contracts shall be awarded by ordinance. In all advertisements for proposals, the quantity and quality of articles shall be fully stated, and any bidder may bid separately for any article named. The award as to each article shall, in all cases, be made to the lowest bidder for such article, and where a bid embraces more than one article, the Supervisors shall have the right to accept or reject such bid or the bid for any one or more articles embraced therein. The Supervisors shall require bonds with sufficient sureties for the faithful performance of every contract. The Clerk of the Supervisors shall furnish printed blanks for all such proposals, contracts and bonds. All bids shall be sealed and delivered by the bidder to the Clerk of the Supervisors, and opened by the Board at an hour and place to be stated in the advertisement for proposals, in the presence of all bidders who attend, and the bidders may inspect the bids. All bids with alterations or erasures therein shall be rejected.

Sec. 2. All contracts for official advertising shall be let annually in like manner by the Supervisors to the lowest responsible bidder publishing a daily newspaper in said city and county which has a *bona fide* daily circulation of at least eight thousand copies and has been in existence at the time of letting said contract at least two years. The award shall in all cases be made to the bidder making the lowest bid. All said advertising shall be printed in type not larger than that known as agate, and with no display heading greater than half an inch in length, and shall be set solid.

In inviting proposals therefor, said advertising shall not be classified, and no proposal shall be acted upon which offers to do said advertising at different rates for different portions thereof.

Said advertising shall be construed to mean the advertising and publication of all official reports, orders, ordinances, messages, resolutions, notices inviting proposals and all notices of every nature, and all, legal notices and process of every kind, nature, character and description, including all advertising of the Sheriff's office, except only such legal notices and process as are by law issuable out of the office of the County Clerk.

No part or kind of said advertising shall be charged or contracted for at a higher rate than any other part or kind of the same is charged or contracted for, except in the case of the delinquent tax list. Any such overcharge shall be cause for the immediate forfeiture of the contract entered into for such advertising.

The newspaper to which the award of said advertising is made shall be known and designated as the " official newspaper."

The advertising of said delinquent tax list shall be let to the lowest responsible bidder, on a separate bidding from all other official advertising.

No Board, Department, Officer or authority shall make any publication which is not expressly authorized by this Charter, and shall make all publications so authorized in the official newspaper exclusively, unless otherwise expressly authorized by this Charter.

Sec. 3. All contracts for subsistence of prisoners must be given out annually by the Supervisors, at a fixed price per day for each prisoner and person connected with the prison; and the advertisement for proposals published as in the last section provided shall specify each article required, the quality thereof, the quantity for each person, and the existing and probable number of persons to be supplied. All articles of food supplied for the prisons, hospitals or other public institutions must be sound and wholesome, and shall be subject to inspection and rejection by the Health Officer, and by the principal officer of the prison, institution or department for which the same are supplied, and the right to such inspection and rejection must be reserved in the contract therefor.

Sec. 4. Except as otherwise provided in this Charter, the Clerk of the Supervisors shall annually, under the direction of said Supervisors, advertise for proposals for supplying the various Departments, Officers and offices of the city and county with stationery and supplies in the nature of stationery, assessment books, minute books, blank books and the printing of blanks. The contracts for stationery shall be separate from those for printing. The estimates for said supplies shall be based upon the average consumption thereof during the three years next preceding; but the notice for proposals shall require a greater or less quantity to be delivered as the Supervisors may designate, and to be supplied at such times and in such quantities as may be necessary. The advertisement for bids for paper shall state the weight, quality and size of the various kinds required, and that for printing shall enumerate the various letter heads, tax bills, tax· receipts, court notices, and all blanks, papers and documents now used or hereafter required in any and all departments of the city and county government, including the forms, papers and blanks now used or hereafter required by the courts of said city and county. The forms for all printing shall be consecutively numbered, and each form and blank shall be known as No. —— [specifying the number]. Said advertisement shall be published for at least ten days, and must specify each article and the estimated amount thereof required during the period of the contract, and shall require bidders to state the price at which each article will be furnished, printed or manufactured, as the same may be required from time to time during said period, and the amount of the bond that will be required as security for the performance of said contract. No stationery furnished to any officer or Department of the City Government at the expense of the city shall contain the name or names of the officer or officers constituting the head of the Department or Board.. The Clerk of the Supervisors shall have rooms in the New City Hall for the custody of such stationery, and when purchased the same shall be delivered to him, and he shall issue and distribute the same to the various departments as required. He shall keep accounts in detail, charging himself with all goods received, and crediting himself with the goods delivered upon order or requisition, as hereinafter provided. When any of such supplies are required for any Department of the city government, said Clerk shall issue the same after the requisition for such articles has been made by the head of a department or his chief deputy, certifying under oath that the supplies named in said requisition are needed for his office. All requisitions for printing shall be made in a similar manner, and when so made, the Clerk shall issue to the contractor for printing, the paper necessary for the execution of the work. Such printing, when completed, shall be delivered to the Clerk, who shall receipt therefor, and deliver the same to the Department for which said printing was done, taking a receipt therefor from the head of the department or his chief deputy. The Clerk shall report monthly in writing to the Supervisors, in detail, the amount of all paper, blanks, books, stationery and printing ordered by and delivered to any Department or Officer.

SEC. 5. Any Officer of said city and county, or of any Department thereof, who shall aid or assist a bidder in securing a contract to furnish labor, material or supplies, at a higher price or rate than that proposed by any other bidder, or who shall favor one bidder over another, by giving or withholding information, or who shall wilfully mislead any bidder in regard to the character of the material or supplies called for, or who shall accept material or supplies of a quality inferior to that called for by the contract, or who shall knowingly certify to a greater amount of labor performed than has been actually performed, or to the receipt of a greater amount or different kind of material or supplies than has been actually received, shall be deemed guilty of misdemeanor. and shall be removed from office.

SEC. 6. All contracts must be in writing and executed in the name of the city and county by the Officer authorized to make the same, and in cases not otherwise directed by this Charter or by law, such contract shall be executed by the Mayor. All contracts must be countersigned by the Auditor, and registered by number and date in a book kept by him for that purpose. When a contractor fails to enter into the contract awarded to him or to perform the same, new bids must be invited, and a contract awarded as provided herein in the first instance. When the Supervisors believe that the prices bid are too high, or that bidders have combined together, to prevent competition, or that the public interest will be subserved, they may reject any and all bids and cause the notice for proposals to be re-advertised.

Sec. 7. No contract for lighting streets, public buildings, places or offices shall be made for a longer period than one year, nor shall any contract to pay for gas, electric light or any illuminating material at a higher rate than the minimum price charged to any other consumer, be valid. Demands for lighting public buildings shall be presented monthly to the Board or Department using or having charge thereof, and shall specify the amount of gas, electric light, or illuminating material consumed in such building during the month.

Sec. 8. When water is supplied by any person or corporation to said city and county, or to any Department, it shall not be paid for at more than the rate for the year established by the Supervisors.

ARTICLE III.

Finance and Revenue.

Chapter I.

OF THE LEVYING OF TAXES.

Section 1. On or before the last Monday of May in each year the Auditor shall transmit to the Supervisors, accompanied with the estimates and reports of each Department, an estimate of the probable necessities of the city and county government for the next ensuing fiscal year, stating the amount required to meet the interest and sinking funds for all outstanding funded debts, together with the amount needed for salaries and the probable wants of all the Departments of the municipal government in detail, and showing specifically the necessities of each specific fund in the Treasury. Such estimate shall also show what amount of income and revenue will probably be collected from fines, licenses, and other sources of revenue, exclusive of taxes, upon property, and what amount will probably be required to be levied and raised by taxation, in order to meet the necessities of said fiscal year. The fiscal year of the city and county shall be the same as that of the State.

Sec. 2. On or before the fourth Monday of June in each year the Supervisors shall levy the amount of taxes for city and county purposes required to be levied upon all property not exempt from taxation. Said amount shall be such as the Supervisors deem sufficient to provide for the payment, during the ensuing fiscal year, of all demands upon the Treasury authorized to be paid out of the same; but such levy, exclusive of the State tax and the tax to pay the interest and maintain the sinking funds of the bonded indebtedness of said city and county, and exclusive also of a tax of not more than ten cents on the one hundred dollars for the construction of the New City Hall until the same is completed, and of a tax of not more than five cents on the one hundred dollars for the construction and repair of other public buildings, and of a tax of two cents on the hundred dollars of valuation for the support and maintenance of the Public Library shall not exceed the rate of one dollar on each one hundred dollars valuation of the property assessed. The Supervisors, in making their said levy, shall apportion the taxes so levied to the several specific funds provided for in this Charter, according to their estimate of the necessities of each of said specific funds.

In making said apportionment, the Supervisors shall take into account and apportion to said funds the income and revenue estimated to arise during the year from licenses, fines and other sources; but the income to pay the interest on the bonded indebtedness and provide for the sinking funds shall always be provided for out of the tax upon property.

The Supervisors shall authorize the disbursement of the public moneys, except those in the Common School Fund, and as otherwise specifically provided for in this Charter for the purposes specified and provided for in the Chapter creating and regulating the various specific funds in the Treasury, and at the close of each fiscal year, if all demands against each specific fund have been respectively paid or satisfied, and all disputed or contested demands finally adjudicated, they shall direct the Treasurer to transfer all surplus moneys to a special fund to be called the Surplus Fund, except such surplus moneys as are in the several Interest and sinking funds, in the Common School Fund, in the Police Relief and Pension Fund, in the Firemen's Relief and Pension Fund, and in such other funds the disposition of whose surplus moneys is in this Charter otherwise provided for.

SEC. 3. The limitation in the preceding section upon the rate of taxation shall not apply in case of any great necessity or emergency; but in such case, such limitation may be temporarily suspended so as to enable the Supervisors to provide for such necessity or emergency; but no increase shall be made in the rate of taxation authorized to be levied in one year, unless such increase be authorized by ordinance passed by the unanimous vote of all members elected or appointed to the Board of Supervisors, and entered in the Journal of the said Board. The character of such necessity or emergency shall be recited in the ordinance authorizing such action, and such ordinance must be approved in writing by the Mayor. Nothing in this section shall authorize the incurring of liabilities against the Treasury not allowed by law, or which cannot be paid out of the income and revenue provided, collected and paid into the proper specific fund as its proportion of the same for such fiscal year, or permit liabilities or indebtedness incurred in any one fiscal year to be a charge upon or paid out of the income or revenue of any other fiscal year.

SEC. 4. In estimating the amount necessary to carry on the government for any fiscal year, and determining and fixing the requirements of the various specific funds of the Treasury, for the purpose of making the annual tax levy, the Supervisors shall keep a record of their proceedings showing in detailed items what money they intended to raise, and for what purposes; and every item of proposed expenditure shall either be applied to the purpose for which it was raised, or shall not be expended during such fiscal year, but shall become part of the Surplus Fund at the end of said fiscal year.

CHAPTER II.

OF THE SEVERAL FUNDS.

SECTION 1. The income and revenue paid into the Treasury shall be at once apportioned to and kept in separate specific funds, as hereinafter provided, and it shall not be lawful to transfer money from one fund to another, or use the same in payment of demands upon another specific fund. The provisions of this section shall not apply to fees paid into the Treasury and placed temporarily to the credit of the unapportioned Fee Fund under the provisions of Chapter III. of this article.

Sec. 2. The several Interest and Sinking Funds in the Treasury authorized by law at the time this Charter takes effect shall continue therein so long as there shall be occasion therefor; and the moneys therein, or which may belong thereto, shall not be used or appropriated for any purpose other than that for which the same were raised.

Sec. 3. The Common School Fund shall consist of all moneys received from the State School Fund; of all moneys arising from taxes which shall be levied annually by the Supervisors for Common School purposes; of all moneys arising from the sale, rent or exchange of any Common School property; and of such other moneys as may from any source be paid into the Common School Fund.

Out of said Fund shall be paid all sums necessary for the purchase, rent and improvement of school sites; for the construction, alteration and repair of school buildings; for the rent and furnishing of school buildings; for the discharge of incumbrances on school property; for the salaries and wages of the Superintendent, teachers, officers and employees connected with the Common Schools, and of other persons who may be employed in the School Department; for supplying the Common Schools with lights, fuel, water, apparatus and necessary school appliances, and for such other expenses of the School Department as are necessary for the maintenance and proper conduct of said Common Schools.

Sec. 4. The Police Fund shall consist of the moneys annually apportioned to said Fund, and of such other moneys as may from any source come into said Fund.

Out of said Fund shall be paid the salaries of the Police Commissioners, the Judges of the Police Court, and of the regular police force, and all sums necessary for providing police stations, implements and appliances, and such amount of money for the contingent expenses of the Police Department, not exceeding in any one year the sum of ten thousand dollars, as the Supervisors shall deem necessary.

SEC. 5. The Street Light Fund shall consist of the moneys annually apportioned to said Fund.

Out of said Fund shall be paid all sums authorized to be paid for lighting the streets, and such public buildings, offices and institutions as are not specially provided to be maintained out of some other specific fund.

SEC. 6. The Street Department Fund shall consist of the moneys arising from taxes annually levied and apportioned to said Fund, and all other moneys which may from any source come into said Fund.

Out of said Fund shall be paid all sums authorized to be paid for repairing and improving streets and the crossings thereof which shall have been accepted so as to become a charge upon said city and county; for cleaning streets, crossings and sewers; for all street work in front of, or assessable upon, property owned by said city and county or any department thereof or by the Government of the United States; for all repairs upon the public streets deemed of urgent necessity; for all work authorized by the Supervisors upon the recommendation of the Board of Public Works or expended by said Board as immediately essential for the safety of life, limb or property, or necessary for public health, or which cannot be assessed upon private property; and for all other expenditures on the sewers, streets and highways deemed necessary by the Supervisors, and authorized by any provision of this Charter.

SEC. 7. The Sewer Fund shall consist of the moneys which may in any year be apportioned to said Fund.

Out of said Fund shall be paid all sums authorized to be paid for the construction of such general system of drainage as may be devised by the Board of Public Works, and which shall not be chargeable upon private property.

SEC. 8. The Fire Department Fund shall consist of the moneys annually apportioned to said Fund and such other moneys as may from any other source come into said Fund.

Out of said Fund shall be paid the salaries and wages of all officers, members and employees of the Fire Department, the salaries and wages of the officers, members and employees of the Fire Alarm and Police Telegraph, and the salary of the Secretary of the Board of Fire Commissioners; all sums authorized to be paid for sites for engine houses; for the construction, equipment, repair and necessary supplies of engine houses; for the construction and repair of cisterns, for the erection of hydrants, for the purchase and repair of fire engines, hose carts, hook and ladder carriages, and for the purchase of all other apparatus and appliances and things of every nature and description necessary for the extinguishment of fires; for all other things necessarily used in the engine houses and buildings of the Department; for all necessary horses, harness, horse feed and stable supplies; for all necessary material, supplies and labor for the maintenance and operation of the Fire Department Yard and Workshop; for all material and supplies necessary for the maintenance, extension and repair of the Fire Alarm and Police Telegraph; and for offices and necessary furniture and supplies for the Board of Fire Commissioners.

Sec. 9. The Health Department Fund shall consist of the moneys annually apportioned to said Fund and of such other moneys as may come into said Fund.

Out of said Fund shall be paid the salaries of all officers and employees of the Board of Health, and any and all other salaries and expenses incurred in the administration of said Health Department, and not expressly provided to be paid out of some other fund.

Sec. 10. The Hospital and Almshouse Fund shall consist of the moneys annually apportioned to said Fund; of all moneys received from the City and County Hospital and from the Almshouse; and of such other moneys as may come into said Fund.

Out of said Fund shall be paid the salaries of all officers and employees of the City and County Hospital; all sums authorized to be paid for material and supplies required for or used in the maintenance of the City and County Hospital and for the treatment and care of the patients therein; the salaries and wages of the officers and employees of the Almshouse, and all sums authorized to be paid for material and supplies required for or used in the maintenance of the Almshouse and the care and support of the inmates thereof; the salaries and wages of the officers and employees of the Hospital for Contagious Diseases; and all sums authorized to be paid for the maintenance of said Hospital for Contagious Disease.

Sec. 11. The Park Improvement Fund shall consist of the moneys annually apportioned to said Fund; of all moneys accruing from rents of grounds, or permits in the parks, or from public property under the control of the Park Commissioners, or arising from the sale of articles from said parks; and of all moneys coming into said Fund by donation, bequest or otherwise.

Out of said Fund shall be paid all sums authorized to be paid for such material, supplies, tools, machinery, appliances, labor and service, as well as for seeds, plants, vines, shrubs, trees, animals and museums, which the Park Commissioners may procure for preserving, improving and beautifying Golden Gate Park and the other public grounds under the control of said Commissioners.

Sec. 12. The Library Fund shall consist of the moneys annually apportioned to said Fund and of all moneys accruing to said Fund by donation, bequest or otherwise.

Out of said Fund shall be paid all sums necessary for the purchase, lease or improvement of real estate, the construction and furnishing of suitable buildings, the salaries and wages of officers and employees of the Public Library and Reading Rooms, the purchase of books, journals and periodicals, and such supplies as may be used in the maintenance of said Library and Reading Rooms and its branches.

Sec. 13. The New City Hall Fund shall consist of the moneys arising from taxes annually levied and apportioned to said Fund.

Out of said Fund shall be paid all sums authorized to be paid for the material, labor and service necessary for the completion of the New City Hall.

Sec. 14. The Public Building Fund shall consist of the moneys arising from taxes annually levied and apportioned to said Fund.

Out of said Fund shall be paid all sums authorized to be paid for the material, labor and service necessary for the construction and repair of public buildings.

Sec. 15. The Stationery Fund shall consist of the moneys annually apportioned to said Fund.

Out of said Fund shall be paid all sums authorized to be paid for books, blanks, stationery, printing and publishing required by said city and county, or by the officers thereof in the performance of their official duties, and not otherwise provided for.

SEC. 16. The Salary Fund shall consist of the moneys annually apportioned to said Fund and of all fees collected in the various Offices and Departments not specially appropriated to some other Fund.

Out of said Fund shall be paid all salaries not specifically required to be paid out of some other specific fund.

SEC. 17. The Jail Fund shall consist of moneys annually apportioned to said Fund.

Out of said Fund shall be paid all sums authorized to be paid for the maintenance of the City and County Jails, and the inmates thereof, and any public reform school provided by law.

SEC. 18. The City Prison Fund shall consist of moneys annually apportioned to said Fund.

Out of said Fund shall be paid all sums authorized to be paid for the maintenance of the city prison and the inmates thereof.

SEC. 19. The Advertising Fund shall consist of the moneys annually apportioned to said Fund.

Out of said Fund shall be paid all sums authorized to be paid for the advertising of said city and county, and of the several Departments and Officers thereof.

SEC. 20. The Receiving Hospital Fund shall consist of the moneys annually apportioned to said Fund.

Out of said Fund shall be paid all sums authorized to be paid for the maintenance and support of the City Receiving Hospital.

SEC. 21. The Election Fund shall consist of the moneys annually apportioned to said Fund.

Out of said Fund shall be paid all sums authorized to be paid for the expenses of election and the registration of voters, except the salaries of permanent officers, which shall be paid out of the Salary Fund.

SEC. 22. The Water Supply Fund shall consist of the moneys annually apportioned to said Fund.

Out of said Fund shall be paid all sums authorized to be paid for water supplied and furnished to the city and county government, and to the several branches, departments, buildings, squares and parks thereof, except Golden Gate Park, the water supplied to which shall be paid for out of the Park Improvement Fund.

SEC. 23. The Police Relief and Pension Fund shall consist of the moneys annually apportioned to said fund.

Out of said fund shall be paid all sums authorized to be paid in the manner provided by this Charter to members of the police force for relief and pensions.

SEC. 24. The Firemen's Relief and Pension Fund shall consist of the moneys properly belonging to said fund, or annually apportioned thereto.

Out of said fund shall be paid all sums authorized in the manner provided in this Charter to be paid to members of the Fire Department for relief and pensions.

SEC. 25. If the Supervisors appropriate money for any other purpose besides those enumerated in this Chapter, it shall at once, when paid into the Treasury, be apportioned to and kept in a separate specific fund, which said Fund shall receive an appropriate designation and shall consist of the moneys apportioned to or paid into the same; and out of said fund shall be paid only such demands as are properly chargeable thereto within the purposes of such appropriation.

SEC. 26. The Surplus Fund shall consist of the money remaining at the end of any fiscal year in any other specific fund, except the Common School Fund and other specific funds as are by this Charter otherwise expressly provided for, after all valid demands, indebtedness and liabilities against such other specific funds incurred within such fiscal year have been paid and discharged; *provided*, that all disputed or contested claims payable out of such specific funds have been finally adjudicated.

Said surplus fund shall be used for the purposes and in the order following:

1st. In payment of any final judgment against said city and county; but no judgment shall be deemed final until passed upon finally by the Court of last resort.

2d. In liquidation and extinguishment, under such regulations as the Supervisors may adopt, of any outstanding funded debt of said city and county.

3d. To be carried over and apportioned among the specific funds and used in the ensuing fiscal year as part of the income and revenue thereof.

SEC. 27. The Special Deposit Fund shall consist of all moneys paid into Court and deposited with the Treasurer by the County Clerk; of all moneys received by the Public Administrator and deposited by him with the Treasurer; and of all other moneys deposited with the Treasurer on special deposit.

The moneys in said fund shall be paid out in the manner prescribed by law; but all demands against said Fund must be allowed by the Auditor in the manner required in other cases.

SEC. 28. Any moneys remaining at the end of any fiscal year in the Common School Fund, the Street Department Fund, the Park Improvement Fund, the Library Fund, the New City Hall Fund, the Police Relief and Pension Fund, the Firemens' Relief and Pension Fund, and the Public Building Fund, shall be carried forward to said respective funds for the ensuing fiscal year; but when the New City Hall shall be completed the surplus money in the New City Hall Fund shall be transferred to the Surplus Fund and thereafter the said New City Hall Fund shall cease.

SEC. 29. Any demand against the Treasury or against any fund thereof remaining unpaid at the end of the fiscal year for lack of money in the Treasury applicable to its payment, may be paid out of any money which may subsequently come into the proper fund from delinquent taxes or other uncollected income or revenue for such year. Such demands shall be paid out of such delinquent revenue, when collected, in the order of their registration.

SEC. 30. Any expenditure contemplated by the Supervisors for any purpose shall be provided for and specifically named in the tax levy; and when collected shall be placed in a specific fund, and used only for such contemplated purpose, and shall be subject in all respects to the rules governing the other specific funds; but nothing herein contained shall be deemed to authorize the raising or expenditure of money unless authorized by law or this Charter.

SEC. 31. When there shall be to the credit of any sinking fund in the Treasury a sum not less than twenty thousand dollars, which may be applied to the redemption of any outstanding bonds to which said fund is applicable, which are not redeemable before their maturity, it shall be the duty of the Mayor, Auditor and Treasurer to advertise for thirty days, inviting proposals for the surrender and redemption of said bonds; and after such advertisement, to award the money in said Sinking Fund, or such portion thereof, as may be required therefor, to the person offering to surrender said bonds for the lowest price; and upon such award, when duly audited, the Treasurer shall, upon the surrender of said bonds, pay the amount to the person to whom the same was awarded; but no bid for the surrender of any of said bonds shall be accepted which shall require a greater sum of money for their redemption than the present worth of the principal and interest of said bonds, calculated with interest at the rate of three per centum per annum.

Chapter III.

OF THE CUSTODY OF PUBLIC MONEYS.

Section 1. All moneys arising from taxes, licenses, fees, fines, penalties and forfeitures, and all moneys which may be collected or received by any officer of said city and county or any department thereof, in his official capacity, for the performance of any official duty, and all moneys accruing to said city and county from any source whatever, and all moneys directed by law or this Charter to be paid or deposited in the Treasury, shall be paid into said Treasury; and all officers or persons collecting or receiving such moneys must pay the same into the Treasury; and no officer or person other than the Treasurer shall pay out or disburse such moneys, or any part thereof, upon any allowance, claim or demand whatever.

Sec. 2. Salaried officers of said city and county shall not receive or accept any fee, payment, or compensation whatever, directly or indirectly, for any services performed by them in their official capacity, nor any fee, payment, or compensation, for any official service performed by any of their deputies, clerks, or employees, whether performed during or after official business hours, nor shall any deputy, clerk, or employee of such officers receive or accept any fee, compensation, or payment, other than their salaries as now or hereafter fixed by law, for any work or service performed by them of any official nature, or under color of office, whether performed during or after official business hours.

SEC. 3. Every fee, commission, percentage, allowance, or other compensation whatever, authorized by law to be charged, received, or collected by any officer of said city and county for any official service, except the salary allowed by law, payable from the Treasury of said city and county, must be paid by the person for whom such service is performed to the Treasurer of said city and county, in the manner herein provided.

SEC. 4. It shall be the duty of every officer of said city and county authorized by law to charge, receive, or collect any fee, commission, percentage, allowance, or compensation whatever, for the performance of any official service or duty of any kind or nature, or rendered in any official capacity, or by reason of any official duty or employment whatsoever, to deliver to the person requiring such service or duty a certificate, in writing, signed by such officer, which shall certify the nature of the official service to be performed and the amount of the fee, commission, percentage, allowance, or compensation allowed by law therefor. The person receiving such certificate shall deliver the same to the Treasurer of said city and county, and shall pay to such Treasurer the amount named in such certificate, and thereupon such Treasurer shall deliver to such person a receipt for the money so paid, which shall show the amount of money received, the day and hour when paid, the name of the person paying the same, the nature of the service to be performed, and the name and official designation of the person by whom the service is to be performed; and like entries shall be made upon the stub of such receipt, which shall be kept by such Treasurer. Upon the delivery of such Treasurer's receipt to the officer therein designated, such officer shall deliver to such person a certificate containing the same items as appear in such receipt, and acknowledging the delivery to him of such receipt, and the day and hour the same was delivered to him, and such officer shall thereupon perform the service or duty in such receipt described, as required by law. The Treasurer shall place all such moneys so received by him to a fund to be designated the "Unapportioned Fee Fund," which is hereby created, and shall keep such fund as other funds in the Treasury are kept, and shall be liable on his official bond for all money so received. ·

SEC. 5. The Auditor or other proper officer of said city and county must prepare and deliver, from time to time, to the Treasurer, and to every officer of said city and county, authorized by law to charge any fee, commission, percentage, allowance, or compensation whatsoever, for the performance of any official service or duty of any kind or nature, as many official certificates and receipts as may be required, charging therewith the Treasurer or other officer receiving them. Such official certificates and receipts must be bound into books containing not less than one hundred such certificates or receipts, and numbered consecutively, beginning with number one in each class required for each officer for each fiscal year, and provided with a stub corresponding in number with each certificate and receipt. When the books containing such certificates and receipts are exhausted by the officer receiving them, he shall return the stubs thereof to the Auditor or other proper officer, in whose custody they shall remain thereafter.

SEC. 6. When a receipt as herein provided is issued by the Treasurer of said city and county, he must state therein the date of payment, the name of the person making the payment, and the amount of such payment, and the nature of the service for which the charge is made, and the name and official designation of the officer performing the service, and shall make corresponding entries on the stub of such receipt.

SEC. 7. Whenever any certificate or receipt is issued by any officer of said city and county, other than the Treasurer thereof as herein provided, he shall state therein the day and hour of the delivery to him of the Treasurer's receipt, the nature of the service therein described, and the amount charged therefor, and the name of the person by whom such receipt is delivered to him, and shall make corresponding entries on the stub to which such certificate or receipt is attached.

SEC. 8. On the first day of each month the Treasurer of said city and county must make to the Auditor a report, under oath, of all moneys received by him as provided in this Chapter, during the preceding month, showing the date and number of the certificate on which the money was received, the amount of each payment, and by whom paid, and the nature of the service, and the name and official designation of the officer performing the service; and at the same time, or oftener, if required by the Auditor so to do, exhibit to the Auditor all official certificates received by him during the previous month, and all official receipts remaining in his hands, unused or not issued, at the close of business on the last day of the preceding month.

Sec. 9. On the first day of each month, every officer of said city and county, authorized by law to charge any fee, commission, percentage, allowance, or compensation whatsoever, must make to the Auditor a report, under oath, of all official certificates and receipts issued by him during the preceding month, showing the date and number of each certificate and receipt, to whom issued, the nature of the service for which the charge was made, and the amount of such charge; and must at the same time exhibit to the Auditor, or other proper officer, or oftener, if required so to do, all Treasurer's receipts deposited with him during the preceding month, and all official certificates and receipts remaining in his hands, unused or not issued, at the close of business on the last day of each preceding month.

Sec. 10. Upon receiving the reports prescribed by sections eight and nine of this chapter the Auditor of said city and county, shall examine and settle the accounts of each officer thereof, and apportion such moneys to the fund or funds to which it is appropriated by law, and certify such apportionment to the Treasurer, who shall thereupon transfer from the "Unapportioned Fee Fund" the amounts so certified, and credit each fund entitled thereto with the proper amount so apportioned.

Sec. 11. Every such officer of said city and county, who is by law allowed to charge and collect mileage for the service of process, and for like service, shall, at the end of each month, prepare and deliver to the Auditor of said city and county, a statement showing each process served, the title of the cause, the name of the deputy or other subordinate officer by whom served, the number of miles actually traveled in making such service, the exact day when such service was made, and between what hours of said day, which statement shall be verified by the oath of such officer. Such Auditor of said city and county, shall thereupon have the power, and he is directed to examine such statement, and issue his warrant upon the Treasurer of said city and county, for such amount of money as shall in his judgment fully reimburse such officer for his lawful expenses in making such service, and such warrant shall be paid by the Treasurer without further approval, out of the " Unapportioned Fee Fund," but no extra mileage shall be charged or allowed for service of two or more processes served on the same trip, by the same deputy or deputies, except for extra mileage actually traveled in serving the additional process, and all mileage charged in violation of this section shall be disallowed by the Auditor, and all amounts disallowed for any reason shall be apportioned as other moneys in the " Unapportioned Fee Fund." Any officer of said city and county, who during the preceding month performed any service for which he is expressly authorized by law to employ a person, at a certain or stated per diem fixed by law, to perform such service other than his regular deputies or other assistants, whose salaries are paid from the public treasury of said city and county, and a person is so employed, and a service is actually performed by such person, and the charge therefor has been paid to the Treasurer for the service of the person so employed; such officer shall, at the end of each month, prepare and deliver to the Auditor of said city and county, a statement, showing the case or instance in which such service was performed, and for whom performed, the name of the person so employed, and by whom the service was performed, the amount of the charge therefor, the time actually employed in performing such service, and the dates of the beginning and ending of the period during which such person was so employed in performing such service, which statement shall be verified by the oath of such officer. The Auditor shall thereupon examine such statement, and if he finds the same to be correct, he shall audit and allow the verified demand of such person so employed and performing the service, for the sum or sums so earned by him and paid by him to the Treasurer for such service, and the Treasurer shall pay such demand so audited and allowed, without further approval, out of the " Unapportioned Fee Fund."

SEC. 12. Nothing in this chapter shall be so construed as to apply to any payment required to be made on account of the levy or collection or delinquency of any tax upon property, or any poll tax, nor for any city and county license, but all such moneys shall be paid to and shall be accounted for in the same manner and by the same officers as are required by law and the provisions of this Charter to charge, receive, collect, or account for the same.

SEC. 13. The Mayor, Auditor and Chairman of the Finance Committee of the Board of Supervisors shall, every month, together examine the books of all officers having the collection or custody of public funds, and shall see and count all the moneys remaining in the hands of the Teasurer, and verify the amount of money by weighing or counting the same.

The Finance Committee of the Board of Supervisors shall, on the first Monday in July and January of each year, and at such other times as they may elect, make the same examination of books and count of money, and report the result to the Supervisors.

The failure for one month to perform this duty, unless prevented by unavoidable cause, shall work a forfeiture of office of any officer required to do the same.

SEC. 14. If on such examination any officer is found to be a defaulter, the Mayor shall forthwith take possession of all moneys, books and papers belonging to his office, and a person shall be appointed by him to fill the office for the time being, who shall give a bond in the same amount and take the same oath of office as the officer whose place he is appointed to fill. If the officer charged as a defaulter be acquitted, he shall resume his duties.

SEC. 15. Every demand against said city and county shall, in addition to the other entries and indorsements upon the same required by this Charter, show the ordinance or authorization under which the same was allowed; the name of the board, department or authority authorizing the same; the fiscal year in which the same was incurred, and the name of the specific fund out of which the demand is payable. Each demand shall have written or printed upon it a statement that the same can be paid only out of the income and revenue provided, collected and paid into the proper specific fund in the

Treasury for the fiscal year in which it was incurred, and shall refer to Chapter II of this Article; and be numbered with reference to the specific fund out of which it is payable, and also to the fiscal year in which it was incurred. A new numbering of all demands shall commence with each fiscal year.

Chapter IV.

OF THE PAYMENT OF CLAIMS.

SECTION 1. The salaries and compensation of all officers, including policemen and employees of all classes, and all teachers in common schools, and others employed at fixed wages, shall be payable monthly. Any demand on the Treasury accruing under this Charter shall not be paid, but shall be forever barred by limitation of time, unless the same be presented for payment, properly audited, within one month after such demand became due and payable; or, if it be a demand which must be passed and approved by the Supervisors or Board of Education, or by any other Board, then within one month after the first regular meeting of the proper Board held next after the demand accrued; or, unless the Supervisors shall, within six months after the demand accrued as aforesaid, on a careful examination of the facts, resolve that the same is in all respects just and legal, and that the presentation of it, as above required, was not in the power either of the original party interested, or his agent, or the present holder; in which case they may by ordinance revive such claim; but it shall be barred in the same manner unless presented for payment within twenty days thereafter. No action of the Supervisors upon any. claim shall make the same payable out of any moneys not arising from the income and revenue of the fiscal year in which the said claim was incurred; nor shall any otherwise valid demand incurred subsequent to the claim which is so revived, be rendered invalid by reason of such revival exhausting the fund out of which subsequent claims might otherwise be paid; but such revived claim shall take date and place as of its revival, and not prior to the ordinance of revival.

ARTICLE IV.

Executive Department.

CHAPTER I.

OF THE MAYOR.

SECTION 1. The chief executive officer of the City and County of San Francisco shall be designated the Mayor. He shall hold his office for the period of two years. He may appoint a Secretary, who shall hold his position at the pleasure of the Mayor.

SEC. 2. He shall vigilantly observe the official conduct of all public officers, and take note of the fidelity and exactitude, or the want thereof, with which they execute their duties and obligations, especially in the collection, custody, administration and disbursement of the public funds and property; and the books, records and official papers of all departments, officers and persons in the employ of the city and county, shall at all times be open to his inspection and examination. He shall take special care to see that the books and records of the said departments, boards, offices and persons, are kept in legal and proper form, and any official defalcation or willful neglect of duty, or official misconduct, which he may discover or which shall be reported to him, shall be laid by him before the Board of Supervisors and the Grand Jury or District Attorney, in order that the public interests shall be protected, and the person in default be proceeded against according to law. He shall from time to time give the Supervisors information in writing relative to the state of the city and county, and shall recommend such measures as he may deem beneficial to its interests. He shall see that the laws of the State and ordinances of the city and county are observed and enforced. He shall appoint a competent person, or persons, expert in matters of bookkeeping and accounts, to examine the books, records, condition and affairs of every department, board or officer, at least once in every six months, and enforce such examination. Any person refusing to submit or permit such examination, or purposely delaying or impeding the same, may be suspended from office by the Mayor, and removed, as in this Charter provided. He shall have a general supervision over all the departments and public institutions of the city and county, and see that they are honestly, economically and lawfully conducted. He shall take all proper measures for the preservation of public order and the suppression of all riots and tumults, for which purpose he is authorized and empowered to use and command the police force, and if such police force is insufficient, it shall be his duty to call upon the Governor for military aid, in the manner provided by law, in order that such riots, or tumults, may be promptly and effectually suppressed, and shall perform such other duties as may be assigned to him elsewhere in this Charter.

SEC. 3. He shall see that all contracts and agreements with the city and county are faithfully kept and fully performed, and that all franchises granted to any person, company or corporation are not violated or disregarded, and to that end shall cause legal proceedings to be commenced and prosecuted, in the name of said city and county, against all persons or corporations failing to fulfill their agreements or contracts, either in whole or in part. It shall be the duty of every officer and person in the employ or service of said city and county, when it shall come to his knowledge that any contract or agreement with the city and county, or with any officer or department thereof, or relating to the business of any office, has been or is about to be violated by the other contracting party, forthwith to report to the Mayor all facts and information within his possession concerning such matter; and a willful failure so to do shall be cause for the removal of such officer or employee. The Mayor shall give a certificate, on demand, to any person reporting such facts and information, that he has done so, which certificate shall be evidence in exoneration from a charge of neglect of such duty. It shall furthermore be the duty of the Mayor to institute such actions or proceedings as may be necessary to revoke, cancel or annul all franchises that may have been granted by the city and county to any person, company or corporation which have been forfeited in whole or in part, or which, for any reason, are illegal and void, and not binding upon the city.

SEC. 4. The Mayor shall appoint all officers whose

election or appointment is not otherwise specially provided for in this Charter or by law, and shall fill all vacancies, and such appointees shall serve for the unexpired term.

SEC. 5.   When an audited demand has been presented to the Treasurer, and not paid, and such fact be made known to the Mayor, he shall immediately investigate the cause of such non-payment, and if he ascertain that the demand has been illegally or fraudulently approved, or allowed, he shall cause the officer guilty of such illegal or fraudulent approval or allowance to be suspended and proceeded against for misconduct in office.   If he ascertain that the demand has been duly audited, and that the Treasurer has moneys applicable to the payment thereof, the Treasurer shall be proceeded against for misconduct in office.   If he ascertain that the demand was not paid for want of money, he shall cause the Tax Collector or other officer who ought to have collected or paid the money into the Treasury, if he has been negligent therein, to be proceeded against for misconduct in office.

SEC. 6   When any person shall furnish to the Mayor a statement, in writing under oath, to the effect that he has cause to believe, that any deputy, clerk or employee under any officer, or in any Department, is incompetent or inefficient, or that there are more deputies than are necessary, the Mayor shall at once investigate the matter, after notice to such deputy, clerk or employee, and his principal, or the head of the Department, and if the Mayor find the same to be true, he shall cause such deputy, clerk or employee to be removed.

SEC. 7.   The Mayor shall be *ex officio* President of the Board of Supervisors, and may call sessions of the Supervisors, and shall communicate to them in writing when assembled, the objects for which they have convened; and their actions at such sessions shall be confined to such objects.

SEC. 8.   When and so long as the Mayor is temporarily unable to perform his duties, a member of the Board shall be chosen President *pro tem.*, and shall act as Mayor *pro tem.*   When a vacancy occurs in the office of the Mayor, it shall be filled for the unexpired term by the Supervisors, and any person possessing the necessary qualifications may be chosen Mayor at such election.

A Supervisor during the term for which he shall have been elected or appointed, shall be ineligible to fill such vacancy.

Sec. 9. The Mayor shall not receive for any public service rendered by him during his term of office any other or greater compensation than the salary allowed him as Mayor.

Chapter II.

THE AUDITOR.

Section 1. The head of the Finance Department of the City and County of San Francisco shall be designated the Auditor. He shall hold his office for the period of two years. The Auditor must be always acquainted with the exact condition of the Treasury and every demand upon it. He shall be in personal attendance at his office daily during office hours, and shall not engage in any other occupation or calling, while Auditor. He shall be the general accountant of said city and county, and shall receive and preserve in his office, all accounts, books, vouchers, documents and papers relating to the accounts and contracts of said city and county, its debts, revenues, and other financial affairs. He shall give information as to the exact condition of the Treasury, and every fund thereof, when requested by the Mayor, the Supervisors thereof, or any committee or members demanding the same.

Sec. 2. The Auditor shall appoint a deputy who shall be designated Deputy Auditor, four clerks and such additional clerks and assistants as the Board of Supervisors may from time to time by ordinance authorize. He shall possess the qualifications required for Auditor. In case of the absence of the Auditor from his office, the Deputy Auditor shall have the same powers in the allowance and approval of demands upon the Treasury, as are authorized to be exercised by the Auditor.

Sec. 3. The Auditor shall adopt a mode of double entry bookkeeping, and keep all accounts general and special, in a systematic, chronological and orderly manner. He shall keep an account of all moneys paid into and out of the Treasury, and the Treasurer shall pay no money out of the Treasury, upon any pretext, except upon demands duly audited and allowed by the Auditor ; and any ordinance or law providing for the payment of any demand, out of the Treasury or any fund thereof, whether from public funds or from private funds deposited therein, shall always be construed as requiring the auditing of such demand by the Auditor before the same be paid.

SEC. 4. He shall number and keep an official record of all demands audited by him, showing the number, date, amount, name of the original holder, on what account allowed, out of what fund payable, and if previously approved or allowed, by what Officer, Department or Board it has been so approved or allowed. It shall be misconduct in office for the Auditor to deliver a demand, with his official approval until this requirement shall have been complied with.

SEC. 5. He shall keep publicly posted in his office, a list of all persons receiving salaries or wages from the city and county, with the amount of monthly salary or wages received, by each, opposite his name, which list shall be revised and corrected by him monthly, and be at all times open to public examination.

SEC. 6. The term "Audited" as used in this Charter, means that the demand has been presented to and passed upon by every Officer, Board, Department and Committee, required to act thereon, and finally allowed, as required by this Charter.

SEC. 7. No demand shall be allowed by the Auditor in favor of any corporation or person in any manner indebted to said city and county, except for taxes not delinquent, without first deducting the amount of any indebtedness, of which he has written notice; or in favor of any person having the collection, custody, disbursement of public funds, unless his account has been presented, passed, approved and allowed, as herein required or in favor of any officer who has neglected to make his official returns or reports in the manner and at the time required by law, ordinance, or the regulations of the Supervisors ; or in favor of any officer who has neglected or refused to comply with any of the provisions of law regulating his duties, on being required by the Mayor, in writing, to comply therewith ; or in favor of any officer or employee for the time he shall have absented himself without legal cause from the duties of his office during office hours ; and the Auditor must always examine on oath any person receiving a salary from said city and county, touching such absence.

Moneys placed in the Special Deposit Fund shall not be subject to the provisions of this section.

SEC. 8. If any person feel aggrieved by the decision of the Auditor in the rejection of, or refusal to approve or allow, any demand presented by such person, he may appeal from such decision to the Supervisors, and their decision thereon shall be final, if such decision be expressed by the affirmative vote of not less than eight members of the Board. If, on such appeal the demand be approved, for the whole or any part thereof, it shall thereafter be presented to the Auditor and entered in the proper book in like manner as other demands allowed by him, and an endorsement must be made of its having been so entered, before it can be paid. In all such appeals the opinion of the City Attorney thereon must be required by the Supervisors.

SEC. 9. Every demand upon the Treasury, except the salary of the Auditor, must before it can be paid, be presented to the Auditor, who shall satisfy himself whether the money is legally due, and its payment authorized by law, and out of what fund it is payable. If he allow it, he shall endorse upon it the word "Allowed," with the name of the fund out of which it is payable, and the date of such allowance, and sign his name thereto. No demand shall be approved, allowed, audited or paid unless it specify each special item, date and amount composing it, and refer by chapter and section to the provisions of this Charter authorizing the same.

SEC. 10. The demand of the Auditor for his monthly salary shall be audited and allowed by the Mayor. All other demands on account of salaries fixed by law, ordinance or this Charter, and made payable out of the Treasury, may be allowed by the Auditor without any previous approval. All demands payable out of the Common School Fund must, before they can be allowed or paid, be previously approved by the Board of Education. Demands payable out of the Treasury for salary, wages, or compensation of deputies, clerks, assistants or employees, in any office or department, must, before they can be audited or paid, be first approved in writing by the Officer, Board, Department or authority, under whom, or in which such demand originated. All other demands payable out of any funds in the treasury, must, before they can be allowed by the Auditor, or recognized, or paid, be first approved by the Department, Board or Officer, in which the same has originated, and in all cases must be approved by the Supervisors.

SEC. 11. The Auditor shall keep an official register of all demands presented to him, for allowance against the various specific funds in the treasury, entering them therein as soon as presented, and numbering them in the order of their presentation as to each specific fund; said register shall show the special number of the demand as acted upon by the Supervisors or the Board, Department or authority authorizing the same. The Auditor shall act upon and allow or reject each demand in the order of its registration. He shall not allow any demand out of its order or give priority to one demand over another drawn upon the same specific fund, unless such demand be entitled thereto. The Supervisors shall, by ordinance, designate the number of assistants and employees necessary to conduct the office of Auditor.

CHAPTER III.

OF THE TREASURER.

SECTION 1. There shall be a Treasurer of the City and County of San Francisco, who shall hold his office for the period of two years. He shall appoint and discharge at pleasure, not to exceed five clerks and assistants, and such additional clerks and assistants from time to time as the Board of Supervisors may, by ordinance, authorize.

SEC. 2. It shall be the duty of the Treasurer to receive and safely keep all moneys which shall be paid into the Treasury, either as the money of said city and county, or of any person, or upon any trust, or for any purpose, and shall not loan, exchange, use or deposit the same, or any part thereof, to or with any bank, banker or person; or pay out any part of said moneys, except upon demands authorized by law and this Charter, and after they shall have been audited by the Auditor. At the close of business each day he shall take an account of and enter into the proper book the exact amount of money on hand, and at the end of every month he shall make and file with the Mayor and publish a statement of all receipts into and payments from the Treasury, and on what account, and from what fund. If he violate any of the provisions of this section he shall be guilty of misconduct in office, and be liable to removal; and be proceeded against accordingly. He shall not loan, exchange, or deposit said moneys, or any part thereof contrary to the provisions of this section, or apply the same to his own use, or the use of any other person in any manner, or suffer the same to go out of his personal custody, except in payment of duly audited demands upon the Treasury. He shall keep the money belonging to each fund established, or which may exist under this Charter at any time, separate and distinct, and shall in no case pay demands chargeable against one fund out of moneys belonging to another. He shall be in personal attendance at his office each day between the hours of 9 o'clock in the morning and 5 o'clock in the afternoon.

SEC. 3. For the better security of the moneys in the Treasury, there shall be provided a joint custody safe having two combination locks—neither one of which will alone open the said safe. The Treasurer shall have the knowledge of one combination and the Auditor of the other. The Auditor shall be joint custodian with the Treasurer of all funds in the joint custody safe; but shall have no control over them except to open and close the safe in conjunction with the Treasurer, when requested to do so in his official capacity, and shall not be held responsible on his official bond for any shortage which may occur in the Treasury.

The gold shall be kept in bags containing $20,000.00 each, and the silver in bags containing $1,000.00 each. To each bag shall be attached a tag showing the nature and amount of coin contained therein. Each bag shall be sealed with the seal of each custodian.

There shall be kept in the safe a joint custody book,

showing the amount and description of all funds in said safe, and whenever any amounts are withdrawn or added thereto, the Auditor and Treasurer shall make the proper entry in the joint custody book and initial the same. If on account of sickness or urgent necessity the Treasurer or Auditor is unavoidably absent, then in such case their representatives shall perform their duties. The estimated amount of money required daily for the payment of demands against the Treasury shall be taken from the joint custody safe and kept in another safe to be provided for the security of the daily working capital, which shall be balanced daily at the close of business hours.

Sec. 4. The Treasurer, on receiving any money into the Treasury, shall make out and sign two receipts for said money; said receipts shall be alike, except upon the face of one of them shall appear the word " Original," and upon the face of the other shall appear the word " Duplicate." Said receipts shall be numbered and dated, and shall specify the amount, on what account and from what person or officer received, and into what fund or on what account paid. The Treasurer shall enter upon the stubs of said receipts a memorandum of the contents thereof, and deliver the receipt marked " Original " to the person or officer paying said money into the Treasury, and forthwith deliver the receipt marked " Duplicate " to the Auditor, who shall write upon its face the date of its delivery to him, and charge the Treasurer with the amount specified therein, and file said receipt in his office.

Sec. 5. All officers receiving money from the Treasury for disbursement shall give receipts therefor, which shall be presented to and countersigned by the Auditor. The Auditor, before signing any such receipt, shall number it and make an entry in a book kept for that purpose of the number, date and amount, by whom and in whose favor given, and on what account. No such receipt shall be valid in favor of the person receiving it until presented by the Auditor and countersigned as aforesaid.

Sec. 6. No demand shall be paid by the Treasurer unless it specify each several item, date and amount composing it, and refer by title, date and section to the law, or ordinance or provision of this Charter authorizing the same; but the allowance or approval of the Auditor, or of the Supervisors, or of any Department, Board or officer, of any demand which upon its face appears not to have been expressly made payable out of the funds to be charged therewith, shall afford no warrant to the Treasurer for paying the same.

SEC. 7. Every lawful demand upon the Treasury audited and allowed as in this Charter required, shall in all cases be paid upon presentation, if there be sufficient money in the Treasury applicable to the payment of such demand, and on payment canceled with a punch, cutting the word "Canceled" therein, and the proper entry thereof made; but if there be not sufficient money so applicable, then it shall be registered in a book kept for that purpose by the Treasurer. Such register shall show the special number given by the Supervisors or other authority, and also by the Auditor, to each demand presented, also when presented, the date, amount, name of original holder, and on what account allowed, and out of what specific fund payable. Upon being so registered it shall be returned to the party presenting it, with the endorsement of the word "Registered," dated and signed by the Treasurer; but the registration of any demand shall not operate in any manner to recognize or make valid such demand, if incurred in contravention to any of the provisions of this Charter. The Treasurer shall not give or allow priority in payment of one demand over another drawn upon the same specific fund, or pay demands out of their order to the detriment, delay or injury of the holder of any demand. The Supervisors shall, by ordinance, designate the number of assistants and employees necessary to conduct the office of Treasurer.

CHAPTER IV.

OF THE TAX COLLECTOR.

SECTION 1. There shall be a Tax Collector of said city and county, who shall hold his office for the period of two years. He shall appoint one Chief Deputy Tax Collector, two Assistant Deputy Tax Collectors, ten clerks and assistants, and such greater or less number of deputies, clerks and assistants from time to time as the Board of Supervisors shall, by ordinance, fix, authorize,

SEC. 2. It shall be the duty of the Tax Collector to collect all licenses which may at any time be required by law or ordinance to be collected within said city and county, and all taxes levied upon real and personal property within the city and county, upon the final settlement to be made by him, according to law, or this Charter, he shall be charged with, and shall pay into the Treasury, without any deduction for commissions, fees or charges of any kind or on any account whatever, the full amount of all taxes, assessments and moneys received by him and not previously paid over, including all moneys paid under protest, and for taxes paid more than once, and for street assessments; he shall be charged with, and be debtor to the city and county for the full amount of all taxes due upon the delinquent tax list delivered to him for collection, unless it appear to the satisfaction of the Supervisors expressed by resolution, that it was out of his power to collect the same by levy, and sale of property liable to be seized and sold therefor.

SEC. 3. He shall visit all places of business and examine all persons liable to pay licenses, and see that licenses are taken out and paid for. In the performance of their official duties, he and his deputies shall have the same powers as police officers in serving process, and in making arrests; and may demand the exhibition of any license for the current term from any person, firm or corporation engaged or employed in the transaction of any business for which a license is required; and if such person, firm or corporation shall refuse or neglect to exhibit such license, the same may be revoked forthwith by said Tax Collector.

SEC. 4. The Auditor shall from time to time deliver to the Tax Collector, such city and county licenses as may be required, and sign the same and charge them to the Tax Collector, specifying in the charge the amounts thereof named in such licenses respectively, and the class of licenses, and take receipts therefor; and said Tax Collector shall sign and collect the same. The Tax Collector shall once in every month, and oftener when required by the Auditor, make to the Auditor, a report under oath, of all licenses sold and on hand, and of all amounts paid the Treasurer, and shall also in that regard, comply with the regulations which may be prescribed by the Supervisors, and at the time of making such report, shall exhibit to the Auditor all licenses on hand and the Treasurer's receipts for all moneys paid into the Treasury.

CHAPTER V.

OF THE ASSESSOR.

SECTION 1. There shall be an Assessor of said City and County, who shall hold his office for the period of four years. He shall appoint one Chief Deputy, one Chief Draughtsman, one Assistant Draughtsman, one Field Deputy, one Chief for Real Estate Department and one Assistant for the same, one Chief for Personal Property Department and one Assistant for the same, one Chief for Mortgage Department and one Assistant for the same, and such greater or less number of deputies and assistants as the Board of Supervisors may, from time to time, by ordinance, authorize. During the months of March, April, May and June the Assessor may appoint such additional deputies and clerks for transacting the business of his office during said four months as the Board of Supervisors may, by ordinance, authorize.

SEC. 2. The Assessor shall assess all taxable property within said city and county at the time and in the manner prescribed by the general laws of the State.

CHAPTER VI.

OF THE RECORDER.

SECTION 1. There shall be a Recorder of the City and County of San Francisco, who shall hold his office for the period of two years. He may appoint one Chief Deputy, four Assistant Deputies, and as many clerks, copyists and assistants as the Board of Supervisors may, by ordinance, authorize.

SEC. 2. It shall be the duty of the Recorder to take into his custody and safely keep all books, records, maps and papers deposited in his office, and upon demand and payment of the fees prescribed therefor by law or by ordinance, to furnish to any one applying therefor a copy of any such book, record, map or paper, certified under the hand and seal of his office. He, or his deputies, when any papers are presented for filing or recording, shall write on the margin of each paper so presented the number of folios, the amount paid for recording the same, and shall number consecutively all instruments and documents filed in his office. He shall also perform all other duties at the time and in the manner prescribed by the general laws of the State.

ARTICLE V.

Legal Department.

CHAPTER I.

OF THE SUPERIOR COURT JUDGES.

SECTION 1. The Judges of the Superior Court of the City and County of San Francisco shall have power to appoint not exceeding five interpreters of foreign languages, who shall act as such interpreters in criminal actions and proceedings in all the courts in said city and county, and in examinations before Coroner's juries.

SEC. 2. All requisitions of the said Superior Court for necessary furniture, lights and stationery for use in the court rooms of said Superior Court and in the chambers of said Judges shall be signed by the presiding Judge of said Superior Court and the Judge in whose court room or chambers the same may be needed, and shall be made to the Board of Supervisors and the said Board of Supervisors shall immediately cause the same to be supplied and payment made therefor out of the proper fund.

CHAPTER II.

OF THE CITY ATTORNEY.

SECTION 1. The Mayor shall appoint an attorney and counselor who shall be styled City Attorney, and who shall hold his office for the period of two years. He must be an attorney of the Supreme Court of this State and must have been in the active practice of his profession for at least ten years, five of which next preceding his appointment must have been in the City and County of San Francisco.

SEC. 2. It shall be his duty to prosecute and defend for the said city and county all actions at law or in equity, and all special proceedings for or against the said city and county; and whenever any cause of action at law or in equity or by special proceedings exists in favor of the said city and county, he shall commence the same when directed by the Mayor or the Board of Supervisors so to do. He shall give legal advice to all officers, Boards and Commissions named in this Charter, in writing, when requested so to do by them, or either of them, in writing, upon questions arising in their separate departments involving the rights or liabilities of the said city and county. He shall not settle or dismiss any litigation for or against the said city and county under his control unless ordered to do so by the Mayor and the Board of Supervisors.

SEC. 3. The City Attorney shall take charge of the collection of delinquent taxes, and for that purpose shall have the right to appoint an assistant who shall be a practitioner of the Supreme Court of this State who shall attend to the same. Said assistant shall execute a bond in the penal sum of $5,000, payable to the said city and county, conditioned for the faithful performance of the duties and the payment of the taxes collected by him, into the treasury of the city and county.

SEC. 4. The City Attorney shall keep bound books of record and registry, and of briefs and transcripts used in causes wherein he appears, and shall keep a register of all actions, suits and proceedings in his charge in which the said city and county is interested, and all official written communications by him to any officer, board or department, and all opinions given by him.

SEC. 5. He shall deliver such books and all records, all reports, documents, papers, statutes, law books and property of every description in his possession belonging to his office or to the said city and county, to his successor in office, who shall give him duplicate receipts therefor, one of which he shall file with the Auditor.

SEC. 6. The City Attorney may appoint four assistants in addition to the collector of delinquent taxes, who shall be practitioners in the Supreme Court of this State, and he may also appoint such other employees as may be authorized by the Board of Supervisors. All of said assistants shall be discharged at the pleasure of the City Attorney. The specific duties of such assistants and employees shall be such as shall be prescribed by the City Attorney.

SEC. 7. The City Attorney shall devote his entire time and attention to the duties of his office, and shall accept and engage in no other employment.

CHAPTER III.

OF THE DISTRICT ATTORNEY.

SECTION 1. The District Attorney is the public prosecutor. He must be an attorney of the Supreme Court of this State and have been in the active practice of his profession for at least five years next preceding his election in the City and County of San Francisco.

SEC. 2. He shall attend all courts in said city and county and conduct all prosecutions for public offenses. He must commence actions on all forfeited bail bonds within thirty days after they are declared forfeited, and diligently prosecute the same until the final determination thereof. No action on a forfeited bail bond shall be compromised. In all actions to recover on bail bonds, the District Attorney, when any property is exposed for sale, may bid, and, if necessary, purchase said property for and in the name of said city and county, at a price not exceeding the amount of the judgment recovered on such bond. Said property, when so purchased, shall be held and disposed of by said city and county in the manner prescribed in this charter. He shall perform such other duties as are or may be prescribed by law.

SEC. 3. He may appoint seven Assistant District Attorneys, each of whom must be an attorney of the Supreme Court of this State, and have been in the active practice of his profession for at least five years next preceding his appointment. They shall assist the District Attorney in the performance of his official duties, and at least four of them shall, under his direction, act as prosecuting attorneys of the Police Courts of the city and county. He may also, when so authorized by the Board of Supervisors, appoint such other assistants, clerks and employees as may be needed in the discharge of his duties. All of said assistants shall be discharged at the pleasure of the District Attorney.

SEC. 4. When the District Attorney shall have been

5

credibly informed that any person, criminally injured by another, is likely to die, he shall take the dying statement of such person and immediately reduce the same to writing.

CHAPTER IV.

OF THE PUBLIC ADMINISTRATOR.

SECTION 1. The Public Administrator of the City and County of San Francisco shall be appointed by the Mayor, and shall hold his office for the term of two years. He shall be an officer of the Superior Court, and subject to its orders. He shall administer upon all estates on which the Public Administrator is by law entitled to administer, and shall perform all duties prescribed by law for Public Administrators.

SEC. 2. He shall not employ counsel at the expense of any estate unless the Court, upon a verified petition, setting forth the facts and reasons why it is necessary that he should have the assistance of counsel, and after such notice, as the Court may direct, shall, by an order entered upon the records of the Court, allow him to employ such counsel. The compensation of such counsel, when employed, shall be fixed by the Court and paid out of the assets of such estate.

SEC. 3. All fees, commissions and emoluments allowed by law to the Public Administrator for the administration of estates of deceased persons shall be by him collected and paid each month into the treasury of the city and county of San Francisco, and an account thereof rendered to the Auditor. He shall be allowed, in full for all services, the annual salary herein provided in lieu of all commissions and emoluments. He shall give an official bond in the sum prescribed by this Charter and such additional and special bonds in each case as shall be prescribed by law or by the Superior Court.

SEC. 4. Upon retiring from his office he shall turn over all estates, business, property and assets of estates, and records of office, to his successor.

SEC. 5. He may appoint such clerks and assistants as the Board of Supervisors may, by ordinance, authorize.

Chapter V.

OF THE COUNTY CLERK.

SECTION 1. The County Clerk shall perform such duties as may be by law imposed on County Clerks.

SEC. 2. He shall take charge of and safely keep all books, papers and records, filed or deposited in his office, or which pertain to the courts of which he is clerk; and he shall not allow any papers, files or records to leaves his custody, except when required by a Judge of said city and county, or a Court to be used by him, or in it, or by a Referee. When any of said papers or records are required in any of the courts within said city and county, or before a Referee therein, he shall, without charge, produce the same, under subpœna or order of the Court.

SEC. 3. On the commencement in or removal to, the Superior Court, of any civil action or proceeding, he shall collect from the plaintiff or party instituting the proceeding, the sum of one dollar, for the benefit of the San Francisco Law Library.

SEC. 4. He may appoint one Chief Deputy, forty deputy clerks and twelve copyists, and such other clerks, copyists and assistants from time to time as the Board of Supervisors may authorize by ordinance.

SEC. 5. For copies of papers furnished and certified by him, he shall charge not more than eight cents for each one hundred words. For certifying copies, which are not prepared by him, he shall be entitled to charge fifty cents, and also one dollar an hour for the time exceeding one hour necessarily occupied in comparing such copies. He must certify all papers presented to him which are copies of any document, paper or record, or portions thereof, in his custody.

SEC. 6. All fees herein mentioned shall be paid into the City and County Treasury as provided by law.

Chapter VI.

OF THE JUSTICES' COURT.

SECTION 1. There shall be five Justices of the Peace, who shall hold office for two years, and shall be the Justices' Court for said city and county. Any of said Justices may hold Court, and there may be as many sessions of said Court at the same time as there are Justices thereof. Said Justices shall choose one of their number to be Presiding Justice, who may be removed and another appointed in his place by a vote of a majority of them. In the temporary absence or disability of the Presiding Justice, any other Justice, designated by the Presiding Justice, may act in his place during such absence or disability. Such Court shall be always open, non-judicial days excepted.

SEC. 2. The Justices' Court and the Justices thereof shall have the powers and jurisdiction in civil causes which may be conferred by law upon Justices of the Peace and Justices' Courts in said city and county. They shall not have jurisdiction to try or decide any public offenses whereof the Police Court of said city and county has jurisdiction. Until otherwise provided by law, the provisions of Articles I and III, Chapter 5, of Title 1, Part One of the Code of Civil Procedure, excepting Sections 85, 86, 97, 98, 111 and 115 thereof, as the same are contained in an Act of the Legislature, entitled "An Act to amend Part One of the Code of Civil Procedure, and each and every Title, Chapter, Article and Section of said Part One, and substituting a new Part One to take the place thereof in said Code relating to Courts of Justice and various officers connected therewith," approved April 1, 1880, are hereby made applicable to the Justices' Courts and the Justices thereof, of said city and county, in like manner and to the same extent as if the same had been at length incorporated in and made part of this Chapter.

SEC. 3. All records, registers, dockets, books, papers, causes, actions, judgments and proceedings lodged, deposited, or pending before the Justices' Court of said city and county are transferred to the Justices' Court herein provided for, which Court and the Justices thereof shall have the same power and jurisdiction over them as if they had been in the first instance lodged, deposited, filed or commenced therein.

SEC. 4. The Clerk of the Justices' Court, and the deputy clerks thereof, provided for by law, and such additional clerks and assistants as the Board of Supervisors may by ordinance authorize, shall be appointed by the Mayor. Their duties shall be such as are prescribed by law.

CHAPTER VII.

OF THE POLICE COURT.

SECTION 1. There is hereby created and established in and for the City and County of San Francisco, State of California, a Court to be known as the " Police Court of the City and County of San Francisco;" which Court shall consist of four Judges, each of whom shall hold office for the period of two years. No person shall be eligible to the office of Judge of the Police Court who has not been licensed to practice before the Supreme Court of the State of California, and who has not practiced for five years continuously before his appointment. Any one or more of the Judges may hold Court. The Court shall be divided into departments, to be known as Department Number One, Department Number Two, Department Number Three and Department Number Four, and there may be as many sessions of said Court at the same time as there are Judges thereof. The Judges shall choose from their number a Presiding Judge, who may be removed at their pleasure. He shall assign them to their respective departments, and may assign and transfer cases to the different departments of the Police Court. Any of the Judges may preside in any of the departments, in the absence or inability to act of the Judge regularly assigned thereto. The judgments, orders and proceedings of any session of said Court held by any one or more of the Judges of said Court shall be equally effective as if all the Judges of said Court presided at said session.

The judges must, within one month after this Charter shall have gone into effect, adopt a set of rules of the Police Court, which may be altered from time to time.

SEC. 2. The Police Court of the City and County of San Francisco shall have:

1st. Exclusive jurisdiction of all prosecutions for the violation of city ordinances, or orders of the Board of Supervisors of the City and County of San Francisco.

2d. It shall have concurrent jurisdiction with the Superior Court thereof of all misdemeanors and of the examination of all felonies committed in the City and County of San Francisco.

SEC. 3. Proceedings in said Court shall be conducted in accordance with the laws of this State regulating proceedings in Justices' and Police Courts, and appeals to the Superior Court; and said Court or any of the Judges thereof, shall have the same power in all criminal actions, cases and proceedings as are now, or are hereafter conferred by the general law of the State upon Justices of the Peace; *provided*, that:

1st. It shall be the duty of the Judges of the Police Court to assign as far as possible all jury cases to one department. Any number of jurors may be summoned to act as a panel from which trial jurors shall be drawn. Said panel of jurors shall serve one month in said Court. Any juror serving his full term shall not be again required to serve as juror in said Court for the period of one year. The jurors shall be summoned in accordance with sections 230, 231 and 232 of the Code of Civil Procedure of California.

2d. That no case shall be dismissed or fine imposed until the testimony for the prosecution shall be taken.

3d. That any defendant who neglects to file his statement on appeal within ten days after sentence shall lose his right to appeal, unless good cause for the delay be shown on affidavit. Press of business on the part of defendant's attorney shall not be deemed good cause for delay. Unless the District Attorney shall file amendments to the proposed statement on appeal within five days after the same shall have been filed the proposed statement on appeal shall be the statement on appeal. It shall be the duty of the Judge before whom the case was tried to settle the statement on appeal within five days after the District Attorney shall have filed his amendments to the proposed statement.

4th. Any person who shall solicit or importune a Judge either before or after judgment to dismiss a case, or mitigate a sentence unless the same be done in open court, shall be guilty of a contempt of court.

5th. A complaint in the Police Court may be demurred to on the same grounds allowed by the Code in demurrers to indictments or informations, and the complaint may be amended after a demurrer is sustained by permission of the court.

6th. A defendant in custody shall have the right to be tried before a defendant on bail, and felonies shall be heard before misdemeanors.

7th. It shall be the duty of the Judges of the said

Court to try all cases as speedily as possible, and to refuse continuances after the first calling of a case except upon affidavit showing good cause therefor.

8th. The general sections of the Code of the State of California shall govern the procedure of the Police Court when not contrary to the provisions of this chapter.

9th. No person shall be eligible to be a bondsman for any defendant on trial in the Police Court, or on appeal from a judgment therein, except he take an oath that the property specified in the undertaking is in the City and County of San Francisco, and that he is worth the amount specified exclusive of property exempt from execution, and exclusive of all demands for which he may become liable by reason of the forfeiture of any appeal or bail bonds for which he is surety.

SEC. 4. No person except a licensed attorney of the Supreme Court of the State of California shall practice law in said Court; *provided*, however, that a person accused of crime shall have the right to defend himself.

SEC. 5. The District Attorney of the City and County of San Francisco shall have the conduct, and attend to the prosecution of all actions, cases and proceedings coming before said Court. To that end he shall appoint an Assistant District Attorney for each of the departments of said Court.

SEC. 6. The District Attorney shall also appoint a Warrant and Bond Clerk and three Assistant Warrant and Bond Clerks, at such salaries as shall be fixed by the Board of Supervisors. It shall be the duty of the Warrant and Bond Clerk to keep his office open continuously night and day for the transaction of business; to draw complaints in actions in the Police Court, and approve the same with his written signature; to have the custody of all bail bonds and appeal bonds taken in the Police Court; to examine the sufficiency of every bail bond and appeal bond taken in the Police Court and to make a return thereon, within twenty-four hours after such bond shall have come into his possession, in the following form:

"I,.............,Warrant and Bond Clerk of the City and County of San Francisco, have examined the within bond and find it good in law. I have examined the records of the City and County of San Francisco, and find the property, its owners and incumbrances herein described to be correct according to said records. Signed ...., Warrant and Bond Clerk." The Warrant and Bond Clerk shall also indorse upon the bond the time when it was issued by him or when it came into his possession. The Warrant and Bond Clerk shall have authority to issue bail bonds and appeal bonds when the liability thereof does not exceed two thousand dollars; and to order the discharge from custody of the persons for whom the bonds are issued; he shall also have authority to take cash bail to the extent in any one case of one thousand dollars. The Warrant and Bond Clerk shall be required to account for all moneys received as bail and make a record of the same in the manner now required by law of the Clerks of the Police Court. The power of said clerks to issue bonds and to order the release of prisoners is hereby abolished.

SEC. 7. In the matter of fixing bail and ordering the release of prisoners the Warrant and Bond Clerk shall be subject to the Judges of the Police Court, and any violation of a valid order of any of said Judges shall be a contempt of Court.

SEC. 8. For any failure to keep the office of the Warrant and Bond Clerk open continuously he shall be immediately dismissed from office by the District Attorney, or the Mayor. The Warrant and Bond Clerk and each of his assistants shall execute to the City and County of San Francisco a bond in the sum of ten thousand dollars to indemnify said city and county against loss caused by their malfeasance or gross negligence. The Warrant and Bond Clerk and his bondsmen shall be liable to the City and County of San Francisco for any loss to the city and county caused by his malfeasance or gross negligence, or the malfeasance or gross negligence of his assistants.

SEC. 9. The Supervisors of said city and county shall provide said Warrant and Bond Clerk with a suitable office for the transaction of business, and suitable appliances for the preservation of documents entrusted to his care.

SEC. 10. It shall be a misdemeanor for any person not a Judge of some Court in the City and County of San Francisco, or the Warrant and Bond Clerk ofsaid city and county, to receive bail money for defendants or to order their discharge.

Sec. 11. The Chief of Police shall appoint one or more police officers to attend constantly on each department of said Court to execute the orders and processes of the Court. The Chief of Police shall cause to be made out and delivered to each of the Clerks of the Police Court at of before nine o'clock in the forenoon of every day a calendar of arrests in which the cases shall be assigned in accordance with the rules and regulations established by the Police Judges. Such calendar shall contain all of the cases assigned according to the rules established by the Judges and shall state the offense with which each defendant is charged and whether the defendant is in custody or on bail. If the defendant is on bail the amount thereof must be stated, and whether the bail be cash or a bond. The name of the officer making the arrest must be stated.

Sec. 12. There shall be appointed by the Judge of each department of said Court a stenographer, whose compensation shall be fixed by the Supervisors of the city and county.

Sec. 13. The Clerk of the City and County of San Francisco shall appoint a Clerk for each department of said Court, who shall receive the same salary as the Clerks of the Superior Court. They shall transact the business of Clerks of said Court as now provided by law.

Sec. 14. Any Justice of the Peace, designated in writing by the Mayor for the purpose, shall have power to preside in and hold Police Court, or any department thereof, in the event of the temporary absence or inability of the Police Judges, or either of them; and the Justice so designated to act as Police Judge shall have and exercise all the powers, jurisdiction and authority conferred upon said Court or the Judges thereof.

Chapter VIII.

OF THE SHERIFF.

Section 1. The Sheriff of said city and county shall hold his office for the period of two years. He shall attend in person or by deputy all the Courts in and for said city and county, except the Police Court. He may appoint an under sheriff, a bookkeeper and two assistant bookkeepers, one superintendent and one assistant superintendent of keepers, twelve deputies for serving papers, twelve bailiffs for the Superior Court, one captain, twelve jailers and one cook for the County Jail No. 1, one superintendent and one assistant superintendent, eighteen guards and one cook for the Branch Jail No. 2, one superintendent and one assistant superintendent, one matron, one assistant matron, five guards and one cook for the Branch County Jail No. 3, one commissary for all jails, one driver of the van, one janitor and such additional or less number of deputies, clerks, jailors, guards, or other assistants as the Board of Supervisors may, from time to time, by ordinance, fix and authorize.

SEC. 2. All fees, including keepers' fees, shall be paid into the County Treasury, as provided by law, and he shall perform all such duties as are prescribed by the general law of the State. He shall not charge or receive for keepers' fees or for any advertisement or publication any other or greater sum than that actually paid by him therefor, and he shall file in each action wherein he shall cause any publication to be made a statement signed by him, showing the amount collected and from whom received, as compensation for such publication, and the amount paid by him therefor, with the date thereof, and the person to whom he made such payment. He shall accompany his monthly statement with his affidavit that he has not in any instance charged or received any other or greater sum as keepers' fees, or as compensation for any advertisement or publication made by him, than the sum actually paid for the same.

CHAPTER IX.

OF THE CORONER.

SECTION 1. The Coroner of the City and County of San Francisco shall hold office for the period of two years. In addition to the duties imposed upon him by law, he shall keep a record of all inquests held by him and a copy of all testimony and proceedings thereof.

SEC. 2. He may appoint four deputies, one messenger, one janitor, and such other greater or less number of deputies and assistants as the Board of Supervisors may, from time to time, by ordinance, authorize. He shall also appoint an official stenographer, whose duties shall be to take down in shorthand the testimony and proceedings had at all inquests held by the Coronor, and shall transcribe the same, and said stenographer shall attach his certificate thereto, certifying to its correctness; and said transcript, when so certified to by him, shall constitute and stand as the depositions of the witnesses produced at said inquests.

ARTICLE VI.

Department of Public Works.

CHAPTER I.

OF THE BOARD OF PUBLIC WORKS.

SECTION 1. There shall be a Department of Public Works under the management of three Commissioners, who shall constitute the Board of Public Works, and who shall not engage in any other occupation or calling while members of said Board. Said Commissioners shall be appointed by the Mayor, subject to removal by him, and hold office for four years. Those Commissioners first appointed shall, at their first meeting, so classify themselves by lot that one of them shall go out of office in two years, one in three years, and one in four years.

SEC. 2. Immediately upon their appointment and qualification, said Commissioners shall organize as a Board, and to that end the Mayor shall appoint one of their number as President, who shall hold his office for the term of one year and until his successor is elected. Said Board shall elect a Secretary, who shall not be a member of said Board; and shall establish rules and regulations governing its proceedings, and for the regulation and conduct of its officers, clerks and employees; and may require bonds from any of its subordinates for the faithful performance of their duties. Such bonds must be approved by all of said Commissioners, and be filed with the Auditor.

SEC. 3. The members of the Board shall visit daily its place of business or of meeting, and shall hold special meetings of the Board thereat as often as they may deem necessary. They shall apportion to themselves specific duties to be performed by each member during the intervals between meetings. The regular meetings shall be held on a day and at an hour fixed by resolution entered upon its records, and which shall not be changed except by similar resolution, of which notice shall be published for two weeks. The meetings of the Board shall be public. No order or resolution shall be passed or business transacted involving the approval of bonds, awarding of contracts, appointment of employees, or resolutions of intention recommending work or improvement, except by the concurrent vote of all said Commissioners. No business shall be transacted at a special or adjourned meeting of the Board except such as may by resolution have been made the special order of business for such meeting, or such as may have been under or proposed for consideration at the meeting from which the adjournment was had.

SEC. 4. The Board shall cause to be kept a record of its proceedings, and shall keep copies of all plans, specifications, estimates, contracts, certificates, receipts, surveys, field notes, profiles and of all papers pertaining to the transactions of the Board. It may, when it shall deem it expedient, and shall, when requested by the Supervisors, furnish to them such data or information as may be requested.

SEC. 5. The Secretary of said Board shall keep a record of the transactions of the Board, specifying therein the names of the Commissioners present at the meetings, and giving the ayes and noes upon all votes. No order or resolution shall be valid or have any effect until the same has been recorded at length by the Secretary in the minutes of, and such record approved by, the Board, together with the names of the Commissioners voting for the same. The Secretary shall cause the publication of all notices herein authorized to be published, or which the Board shall order to be published, and shall perform such other duties as the Board may from time to time prescribe or direct.

SEC. 6. Said Board may, from time to time, appoint as many clerks and employees as may be necessary, and as may be by ordinance authorized by the Supervisors.

The salaries of all officers, clerks and employees of said Board, except so far as the same are designated in this Charter, shall be fixed from time to time by the Supervisors on recommendations by said Board.

SEC. 7. Said Board shall immediately after its organization take possession and have the custody and control of all maps, surveys, field notes, records, plans, specifications, contracts, models, machinery, tools, appliances, contract rights, privileges, books, documents, papers, archives, and property belonging to said City and County, heretofore kept by or in the offices of the City and County Surveyor, the Superintendent of Public Streets, Highways and Squares, and the Board of New City Hall Commissioners.

SEC. 8.   It shall be, and is hereby made, the especial duty of the Board of Public Works to prepare, at least three months previous to every city election, an estimate of the value of the various street railroads of San Francisco; the value of the gas, electric or other plants or methods for lighting said city in all portions, both public and private, thereof; the water works of said city; the telephones of said city, and all other franchises granted and in use in such city and county.   The estimate thus made shall be the basis upon which may be submitted to the electors of said city and county the question whether or not said electors desire to purchase such properties, or any of them.

SEC. 9.   After the acquisition by said city and county of any of the properties mentioned in the foregoing section, the Board of Public Works shall take control and appoint all superintendents, engineers or other employees necessary to the proper, efficient and economical management of the same.   The wages of all such employees shall be determined and fixed by the Board of Public Works.

SEC. 10.   Said Board shall have special charge, superintendence and control, subject to such ordinances as the Supervisors may from time to time adopt, of all streets, including Point Lobos avenue and Point Lobos road from Central avenue to the Pacific Ocean, highways, roads, bridges, and public places (except such as are or may be entrusted to the management of the Park Commissioners), belonging to said city and county, or dedicated to public use, and of the improvement and repair thereof; of all sewers, drains and cesspools, and the work pertaining thereto, or to the draining of said city and county; of the cleaning of streets, and of all repairs upon accepted streets; of the construction and repair of all public buildings, and the making of all public improvements for said city and county, or under its authority, and of the repairs to such improvements; of all lamps and lights for the lighting of the streets, parks, public places and public buildings of said city and county, and of the erection of all posts for such lights and lamps; and of all public works and improvements hereafter to be done by said city and county.

Sec. 11.   Said Board shall have exclusive authority to prescribe uniform rules and grant permits, in conformity with the ordinances of said city and county, for the moving of buildings through the streets thereof, and the building or placing of cellars or vaults under the streets or sidewalks; the construction of steps or other approaches to buildings upon the sidewalks, and of railings and fences enclosing areas upon the sidewalks; the laying down and construction of railroad tracks in the streets; the erection of telegraph and telephone poles, and poles for electric lighting, and the laying under the surface of the streets or sidewalks of telegraph or telephone wires, and wires for electric lighting; the construction of drains and sewers; the laying down and taking up of gas, steam and water pipes, pneumatic or other tubes or pipes, and sewers and drains, and determining the location thereof; the using of the street or any portion thereof for the deposit of building material in front of a building during its construction or repair, or for any purpose other than such as ordinarily and properly belongs to the public from the dedication thereof to public use; and without such permission in writing from said Board no person shall do any of the acts in this section enumerated.

Sec. 12.   All electric, telegraph and telephone wires shall be located, laid, erected and maintained, subject to the approval of the Superintendent of the Fire Alarm and Police Telegraph.

Sec. 13.   Said Board shall have full power to regulate and control, subject to the ordinances of said city and county, the manner of using the streets, sidewalks and public places, and to cause the removal of all obstructions therefrom; and to cause the prompt repair of the streets, sidewalks and public places when the same may be taken up or altered.   Said Board is authorized to collect, by suit or otherwise, in the name of the City and County of San Francisco, the expense of such repairs from the person or persons by whom such street or sidewalk was injured or torn up.

Sec. 14. Before granting any permit to any person to make excavations in a public street or streets for the purpose of making repairs or connections with the public sewers, the gas or water mains or any other purpose, the parties applying for such permit shall file with the application a map showing what part of the street or streets is required to be opened and the nature and extent of the excavation to be made, and deposit such amount of money as the Board of Pubic Works shall consider necessary to replace all material excavated, and repair, replank or remacadamize the street where the excavations were made.

The replacing of all material and the replanking or remacadamizing of the street or streets and the removal of surplus material shall in all cases be performed by the Street Department of the Board of Public Works out of the money deposited, and the balance returned to the party making the deposit. All Railroad, Gas, Water, Electric Light, Telegraph, Telephone or other companies, or individuals, before taking up the pavement or in any way disturbing the roadway or sidewalk of any street or streets shall file with the Board of Public Works a map showing the extent and nature of the excavations to be made before permission shall be granted to open the roadway or sidewalk of any street or streets, when the Board shall detail an officer to superintend the replacing of all material and the repaving, replanking or remacadamizing of the streets where the excavations have been made, which must be done under his direction and to his entire satisfaction.

Sec. 15. Said Board shall appoint a Civil Engineer, who shall have had at least ten years practical experience as such, who shall be designated City Engineer. He shall perform all civil engineering and surveying required in the prosecution of the public works and improvements done under the direction and supervision of the Board, and shall certify to the progress and completion of the same, and do such other surveying or other work as he may be directed to do by said Board, or by the Supervisors. He shall possess the same power in said city and county in making surveys, plats and certificates as is, or may be, from time to time, given by law to county surveyors; and his official acts and all plats, surveys and certificates made by him shall have the same validity and be of the same force and effect as are or may be given by law, to those of county surveyors.

Sec. 16. The Supervisors shall, by ordinance, upon the recommendation of said Board, establish such fees and charges as may be proper for the services to be performed by the City Engineer, and as are not inconsistent with the laws of the State, and may, upon like recommendation, from time to time, change and adjust the same. Said Engineer shall require such fee or charge to be paid in advance to the Secretary of the Board for any official act or service demanded of him. With the consent and approval of the Board, the City Engineer may appoint such deputies, not exceeding the number that may be fixed by the Supervisors, as the duties of his office may require. The deputies so appointed shall receive such salaries or compensation as may be fixed by the said Board, and they, or any of them, may be removed at pleasure by the City Engineer, or by said Board.

Sec. 17. Said Board shall appoint an Architect who, under the direction and control of said Board, shall prepare plans and specifications of the work to be done; make necessary drawings and estimates of cost for the same; judge of and determine the quality and durability of the materials that may be furnished for the construction or repair of any public building, and approve of or reject the same, and take special care that all work be done in a good, substantial and workmanlike manner, and in accordance with the drawings, plans and specifications. Upon the completion of the New City Hall, the office of said Architect shall cease.

Sec. 18. Said Board shall appoint a Superintendent of Public Works, who shall be a master builder, and who shall, when any public building is in the course of construction or of repair, or when any materials to be used in its construction or in its repair are being furnished, be in attendance at said building and see that the work is done in a good, substantial and workmanlike manner, and that the materials used or furnished are of the description, quality and quantity called for by the specifications and contract. All work upon public buildings under the control of said Board shall be done under the immediate supervision of said Superintendent, and all material used in the construction or repair thereof, shall be furnished under his immediate supervision. He shall perform such other duties as may be required of him by said Board. He shall devote his whole time to the duties of his office, and shall not be engaged in any other business or receive any salary or compensation for any other service.

SEC. 19. All applications for establishing or changing the grade of any street or streets, the improvement of public grounds or buildings, the laying out, establishing, opening, closing, straightening, widening or improvement of any street, road or highway, or the laying out and opening of any new street through public or private property, and for all public improvements which involve the necessity of taking private property for public use, or where any part of the cost or expense thereof is to be assessed upon private property, shall be made to said Board, and such work or improvement shall not be ordered or authorized until after said Board shall have reported to the Supervisors upon said application.

SEC. 20. All public work, authorized by the Supervisors to be done under the supervision of the said Board, shall be done under written contract, except in case of urgent necessity as hereinafter provided. Before the award of any contract for doing any work authorized by this Article, said Board shall cause a notice to be posted conspicuously in its office for not less than five days, and published for the same time, inviting sealed proposals for the work contemplated; *except*, however, that when any repairs or improvement, not exceeding an estimated cost of five hundred dollars, shall be deemed of urgent necessity by said Board, such repairs or improvement may be made by said Board, by and with the consent of the Mayor, under written contract or otherwise, without advertising for sealed proposals.

SEC. 21. Said advertisement and notice shall invite sealed proposals, to be delivered at a certain day and hour at the office of said Board, for furnishing the materials for the proposed work, or for doing said work, or for both, as may be deemed best by said Board, and shall contain a general description of the work to be done, the materials to be furnished, the time within which the work is to be commenced, and when to be

6

completed, and the amount of bond to be given for the faithful performance of the contract, and shall refer to plans and specifications on file in the office of said Board for full details and description of said work and materials.

SEC. 22. All proposals shall be made upon printed forms to be prepared by said Board, and furnished gratuitously upon application, with a form for the affidavit hereinafter provided for, printed thereon. Each bid shall have thereon the affidavit of the bidder that such bid is genuine, and not collusive or sham; that he has not colluded, conspired, connived or agreed, directly or indirectly, with any other bidder or person to put in a sham bid, or that any other person shall refrain from bidding; and has not in any manner sought by collusion to secure any advantage against said city and county, or any person interested in said improvement, for himself or any other person. All bids shall be clearly and distinctly written, without any erasure or interlineation, and if any bid shall have an erasure or interlineation it shall not be received or considered by said Board. Any contract made in violation of any of the foregoing provisions, and, in the case of improvement of streets, any assessment for the work done under said contract, shall be absolutely void.

All proposals offered shall be accompanied by a check, certified by a responsible bank, payable to the order of the Clerk of the Supervisors, for an amount not less than ten per cent. of the aggregate of the proposal, and no proposal shall be considered unless accompanied by such check.

No person, corporation or firm shall be allowed to make, file, or be interested in, more than one bid for the same work. If on the opening of said bids more than one bid appear in which the same person, corporation or firm is interested, all such bids shall be rejected.

SEC. 23. On the day and at the hour specified in said notice inviting sealed proposals said Board shall assemble and remain in session for at least one hour thereafter, and all bids shall be delivered to said Board while it is so in session, and within the hour named in the advertisement. No bid not so delivered to the Board shall be considered. Each bid as it shall be received shall be numbered and marked "Filed" by the President, and be authenticated by his signature. At the expiration of the hour stated in the advertisement within which the bids will be received, the Board shall, in open session, open, examine and publicly declare the same, and an abstract of each bid shall be recorded in the minutes of the Board by the Secretary. Before adjourning, the Board shall compare the bids with the record made by the Secretary, and shall thereupon, at said time, or at such other time, not exceeding twenty days thereafter, as the Board may adjourn to, award the contract to the lowest bidder, except as otherwise herein provided. Notice of such award shall forthwith be posted for five days by the Secretary of said Board in some conspicuous place in the office of said Board, and be published for the same period of time. The Board may reject any and all bids, and must reject the bid of any party who has been delinquent or unfaithful in any former contract with said city and county, and all bids other than the lowest regular bid; and on accepting said lowest bid, shall thereupon return to the proper parties the checks corresponding to the bids so rejected. If all the bids are rejected, the Board shall return all the checks to the proper parties, and again invite sealed proposals, as in the first instance.

The check accompanying the accepted bid shall be held by the Secretary of the Board until the contract for doing said work, as hereinafter provided, has been entered into, whereupon said certified check shall be returned to said bidder.

• If said bidder fails or refuses to enter into the contract to do said work, as hereinafter provided, then the certified check accompanying his bid, and the amount therein mentioned, shall be forfeited to said city and county, and shall be collected and paid into the proper fund. Neither the Board of Public Works nor the Supervisors shall have power to relieve from, or remit, such forfeiture.

Sec. 24. If at any time it shall be found that the person to whom a contract has been awarded has, in presenting any bid or bids, colluded with any other party or parties, for the purpose of preventing any other bid being made, then the contract so awarded shall be null and void, and said Board shall advertise for a new contract for said work.

Sec. 25. In the case of improvement of streets, the

owners of the major part of the frontage of lots and lands upon the street whereon the work is to be done, or which are liable to be assessed for said work, or their agents, shall not be required to present sealed proposals, but may, upon making oath that they are such owners, or the agents of such owners, within ten days after the first posting of notice of said award, elect to take said work and enter into a written contract to do the whole work at the price at which the same has been awarded. Should said owners not elect to take said work and enter into a written contract therefor within said ten days, or fail to commence the work within fifteen days after the first publication of notice of said award, and prosecute the same with diligence to completion, the Board shall enter into a contract with the original bidder to whom the contract was awarded, and at the price specified in his bid. If said original bidder fail or refuse for fifteen days after the first publication of notice of the award to enter into the contract, the Board shall again advertise for proposals, as in the first instance.

SEC. 26. If the owners or contractor who may have entered into any contract do not complete the same within the time limited in the contract, or within such further time as is hereinafter provided, said Board may relet the unfinished portion of said work, after pursuing the formalities hereinbefore prescribed for the letting of the whole.

SEC. 27. All contracts shall be drawn under the supervision of the City Attorney, and shall contain detailed specifications of the work to be done, the manner in which it shall be executed, and the quality of the material to be used. No change or modification in the plans or specifications shall be made after proposals for doing the work have been called for.

Every contract entered into by said Board shall be signed by all the members thereof, and by the other contracting party. All contracts shall be signed in triplicate, one of which, with the specifications and drawings, if any, of the work to be done, and the materials to be furnished, shall be filed with the Clerk of the Supervisors; one thereof, with said specifications and drawings, shall be kept in the office of the Board; and the other, with said specifications and drawings, shall be delivered to the contractor.

At the same time with the execution of said contract, said contractor shall execute to said city and county, and deliver to the Secretary of the Board, a bond in the sum named in the notice for proposals, with two or more sufficient sureties to be approved by said Board, or shall deposit with the Secretary a certified check upon some solvent bank, for said amount, for the faithful performance of said contract. No surety on any bond shall be taken unless he shall be a payer of taxes on real property, the assessed value of which, over and above all incumbrances, is equal in amount to his liabilities on all bonds on which he may be security to said city and county; and each surety shall justify and make an affidavit (for which a form shall be printed upon said bond), signed by him, that he is assessed upon the last Assessment Book of said city and county in his own name for real property in an amount greater than his liability on all bonds on which he is surety to said city and county, and that the taxes on said property so assessed are not delinquent.

The contract shall specify the time within which the work shall be commenced, and when to be completed, as was specified in the notice inviting proposals therefor. Upon the recommendation of said Board the Supervisors may extend said time; but in no event shall the time for the performance of said contract be extended by the Supervisors more than ninety days beyond the time originally fixed for its completion. In case of failure on the part of the contractor to complete his contract within the time fixed in the contract, or within such extension of said time as is herein provided, his contract shall be void, and the Board shall not pay or allow to him any compensation for any work done by him under said contract; and, in the case of improvement of streets, no assessment shall be made for the work done under said contract.

Sec. 28. The work in this Article provided for must be done under the direction and to the satisfaction of said Board; and the materials used must be in accordance with the specifications and be to the satisfaction of said Board, and all contracts provided for in this Article must contain a provision to that effect, and also, that in no case, except where it is otherwise provided in this Charter, will said city and county, or any Department or Officer thereof, be liable for any portion of the expense, or in the case of improvement of streets, for any delinquency of persons or property assessed.

When said work shall have been completed to the satisfaction and acceptance of said Board, it shall so declare by resolution, and thereupon, said Board shall deliver to the contractor a certificate to that effect, which shall be a demand upon the Treasurer.

SEC. 29. The Commissioners of said Board shall not, nor shall either of them, or any person employed in said Department be interested, directly or indirectly, in any contract for work, labor, or material entered into by said Board; nor shall either of such Commissioners, officers or employees, be allowed to receive any gratuity or advantage from any contractor, laborer, or person furnishing labor or material for the same. Any contract made in violation of any of the provisions of this section shall be void; and the receipt of any such gratuity shall be cause for the immediate removal from office, or from employment, of the person so receiving it.

CHAPTER II.

OF THE IMPROVEMENT OF STREETS.

SECTION 1. All streets, lanes, alleys, places and courts in said city and county now open or dedicated, or which may hereafter be opened or dedicated to public use, and of which the grade and width have been legally established, shall be deemed and held to be open public streets for the purposes of this Article.

SEC. 2. Certain streets shall be, and hereby are designated as boulevards; no such street or boulevard shall ever have laid or constructed upon it any street railroad of any manner or mode of construction whatever, or to be propelled by the use of any kind of motive power whatever, and no franchise for the laying or building of any railroad on any such street shall ever be granted.

The following streets are hereby designated as boulevards, as above provided, namely: Fulton street, from the City Hall to Golden Gate Park; Golden Gate avenue; Lombard street, west from Van Ness avenue; Van Ness avenue; Steiner street; and First avenue from Golden Gate Park to the Presidio Reservation.

The Board of Supervisors may, by ordinance, designate other streets as boulevards, upon the recommendation of the Board of Public Works and the consent of a majority of the owners of property fronting on such streets, respectively.

Heavy trucks or other vehicles of any kind for the removal, carrying or hauling of heavy material shall not be allowed to use any street thus designated as a boulevard, or to continue their passage over, or along the same, for the distance of more than one square or block, that is to say, for more than the distance or space between any two next adjacent streets crossing any such boulevard; and, *provided further*, that in addition to the vehicles hereinbefore mentioned, all carriages, wagons or other vehicles for traffic or carrying parcels, or displaying signs, shall be excluded from Golden Gate avenue from Van Ness avenue to Devisadero street, and any such vehicle having business on Golden Gate avenue, between Van Ness avenue and Devisadero street, shall enter Golden Gate avenue through a street next adjacent to the point at which such business is to be transacted and leave the said Golden Gate avenue at one of the two crossings next adjacent to the point at which such business shall have been transacted.

SEC. 3. The cost and expense of all work or improvement done upon any part of said streets, lanes, alleys, places or courts, under the order of the Board, shall be borne and paid as follows, viz.:

First—The City and County shall pay out of the Street Department Fund the cost and expense—

1. Of all work done on streets, crossings and intersections of streets that have been or may be accepted by said city and county, after the acceptance of the same, and of all repairs and improvements deemed of urgent necessity that may be made upon the public streets and highways.

2. Of all work done in front of, or that may be assessed to, property owned by said city and county, or any department thereof.

3. Of all work done in front of, or that may be assessed to, property owned by the United States or the State of California until such time as the cost thereof may be refunded by the said State of California or the said United States.

Second—The cost and expense of all sewers, cesspools,

manholes, culverts and drains, and all grading, planking, macadamizing, paving piling and capping any street, or portion thereof, and of all curbs thereon, shall be assessed upon the lands within the block or blocks adjacent thereto as herein provided.

Third—The expense of all work on such portion of any street required by law to be kept in order by any person, company, or corporation, having railroad tracks thereon, shall be borne and paid for by such person, company or corporation.

No assessment shall be levied upon any property, which, together with all assessments for street improvements that may have been levied upon the same property during the year next preceding, will amount to a sum greater than fifty per centum of the value at which said property was assessed upon the last preceding Assessment Book of said city and county.

SEC. 4. When any street or portion of a street, not less than one block, or any entire crossing, shall have been paved with stone or with such material as may be recommended by the Board of Public Works and approved by the Supervisors by ordinance, throughout the entire width of the roadway thereof, and curbs of stone and sidewalks shall have been constructed thereon, and a brick sewer or iron-stone pipe, or metal pipe, or of other approved material, shall have been constructed or placed therein, under such regulations as may have been adopted by said Board, the same shall be accepted by the Supervisors upon the recommendation of said Board, and all improvement of said streets, except for sidewalks, shall thereafter be done at the expense of said city and county; *provided*, that the Supervisors may, upon the recommendation of said Board, partially or conditionally accept any street or portion of a street, without a sewer, if the ordinance of acceptance expressly states that the Supervisors deem such sewer to be then unnecessary ; but the lots of land previously, or at any time, assessable for the cost of constructing a sewer, shall remain and be assessable for such cost, and for the cost of repairs and restoration of the street damaged in the said construction, when said Supervisors shall deem a sewer to be necessary, and shall order it to be constructed, the same as if no partial or conditional acceptance had been made.

The Supervisors shall not accept any sidewalk, or incur any liability against said city and county for the construction or repair of any sidewalk, except in front of or with respect to public property.

SEC. 5. When application is made to said Board for any work or improvement, the cost and expense of which, or any part thereof, is to be assessed upon private property, the Board shall investigate the same; and if it determine that such improvement is expedient, it shall so report to the Supervisors; and the Supervisors shall not order any such improvement until the same has been recommended by said Board. When the construction of any sewer or drain shall involve a cost of more than five dollars per lineal foot for any block, it shall not be authorized except by an ordinance passed by the affirmative vote of not less than nine members of the Board of Supervisors. If an application is made for any work or improvement of which the cost and expense is to be paid by said city and county, and said Board shall not approve of such application, it shall report to the Supervisors its reasons for such disapproval, and the Supervisors may then, after having obtained from said Board an estimate of the cost and expense of said work or improvement, by ordinance passed by the affirmative vote of not less than nine members of the Board of Supervisors, order the doing of said work, or the making of said improvement.

The Board of Public Works may also, except as herein prohibited, recommend any improvement, the cost and expense of which is to be paid by said city and county, though no application may have been made therefor, and must make, with said recommendation to the Supervisors, an estimate of the expense, and in such case the Supervisors may order the same done.

When said Board shall recommend any work to be done on a street intersection or crossing, where the streets do not intersect each other at right angles, it shall in each such case determine what lots in the blocks adjacent to such intersection or crossing will be benefitted by said work, and shall cause a map to be made on which shall be delineated the lots so to be benefitted. Said map shall be transmitted to the Supervisors with said recommendation.

SEC. 6. Before recommending to the Supervisors the

ordering of any work or improvement, the cost and expense of which, or any part thereof, is to be assessed upon private property, said Board shall pass a resolution of its intention to recommend the same, specifying the work to be recommended, and shall fix a day when it will take final action upon such resolution. Upon the passage of said resolution, and within ten days thereafter, the Secretary of said Board shall, without any further authority, cause a copy of said resolution to be published for a period of ten days (legal holidays excepted), and cause a copy to be deposited in the post office at San Francisco, with postage prepaid, addressed to each person represented on the Assessment Book of said city and county for the next preceding fiscal year as being owner of land liable to be assessed for said improvement; but if said lot stand on said book in the name of unknown owners, such notice need not be sent.

Said Board shall also cause to be conspicuously posted along the line of said contemplated improvement, at points not more than one hundred feet in distance apart, notices, not less than three in all, of the passage of said resolution. Each of said notices shall be headed, "Notice of Street Work," in letters of not less than one inch in length, and shall in legible characters state the fact of the passage of said resolution, its date, and briefly, the work or improvement proposed, and refer to the resolution for further particulars.

Said Board shall not include more that five blocks in any one resolution of intention.

SEC. 7. At any time within ten days after the first publication of said resolution of intention, the owner of, or any person interested in, any lot liable to be assessed for the proposed improvement, may file with the Secretary of said Board his objection to said improvement, stating briefly the grounds thereof; and if at any time within said period of ten days the owners of a majority of the frontage of the lands liable to be assessed for said improvement shall file written objections to the same, the Board shall not recommend the ordering of said improvement, and shall not within three months thereafter pass any resolution of its intention to recommend the same, unless prior thereto, it shall receive a petition therefor signed by the owners of a majority of the frontage of the lands liable to be assessed for said improvement.

Upon the day fixed in its resolution of intention for final action thereon, or at its next regular meeting, the Board shall consider and pass upon said objections. If the Board shall consider that the objections are sufficient it shall adopt a resolution to that effect, and shall not recommend the ordering of said improvement If it shall consider that said objections are not sufficient, or if no objections are filed, the Board may recommend the ordering of said improvement, and must, with its recommendation, transmit to the Supervisors all objections to such recommendation that may have been filed.

At the next regular meeting after receiving from said Board its recommendation of such improvement, or at such time within thirty days thereafter to which the hearing thereof by the Supervisors may be postponed, the Supervisors shall act upon such recommendation; and if any objections to the ordering of such improvement have been transmitted with said recommendation, they shall consider and dispose of said objections before passing upon said recommendation. If the Supervisors shall consider the objections or any of them sufficient, it shall so declare by resolution. If the Supervisors consider the objections insufficient, they may by ordinance order the work or improvement to be done. Their action on said recommendations must in each case be certified by the Clerk of the Supervisors to the Secretary of the Board of Public Works, and such Secretary shall thereupon enter the facts so certified in his records of street work.

Sec. 8. When the work under any contract shall have been completed, the contractor·shall make and file in the office of said Board of Public Works an affidavit to the effect that he has not entered into any private agreement, verbal or written, with any person liable to be assessed for said work, or with any one on his behalf, to accept a price from him less than the price named in said contract, or to make any rebate or deduction to him from such price. Any such agreement shall be deemed a fraud upon all persons liable to be assessed for such work other than the property owners who were parties to the agreement, and shall operate to avoid, as to such persons so defrauded, any assessment made for the work done under such contract.

SEC. 9. When any work in or upon any public street shall have been completed according to contract, and the affidavit mentioned in the next preceding section shall have been made, said Board shall make an assessment to cover the sum due for the work performed and specified in said contract (including all incidental expenses), in conformity with the provisions of this Article, according to the nature and character of the work; which assessment shall briefly refer to the contract, the work contracted for and performed, and shall show the amount to be paid therefor, together with any incidental expenses, the rate per front foot assessed, the amount of each assessment, the name of the owner of each lot (if known to said Board, and if not known, the word "*unknown*" shall be written opposite the number of the lot and the amount assessed thereon); the number of each lot assessed, and shall have attached thereto a diagram exhibiting the street or street crossing on which the work has been done, and showing the relative location of each distinct lot to the work done, numbered to correspond with the numbers in the assessment, and showing the number of front feet assessed for said work. A mistake in the name of the owner shall not invalidate any assessment.

SEC. 10. After making said assessment said Board shall cause notice thereof to be published for five days, and to be delivered to the occupant of each of the lots assessed, which notice shall state the day and hour when the Board will at its office take final action upon said assessment. If any of said lots are unoccupied, said notice shall be posted in a conspicuous place upon said lot or lots, and in all cases a copy of said notice shall be sent by mail, with postage prepaid, addressed to the person in whose name the lot to be assessed stands upon the Assessment Book of said city and county for the next preceding fiscal year, at the post office at San Francisco; but if such lot stands upon said Book in the name of " unknown " owners, no such notice need be sent.

SEC. 11. At any time prior to the time fixed in said notice, any person interested may present in writing and file with the Board his objections to said assessment, stating briefly wherein he deems the same erroneous. At the time specified in said notice, or at some day to which the hearing shall then be adjourned, the Board shall consider said objections, and if it shall deem them well taken, it shall again assess such amount upon said lots and lands as it shall deem to be right, and shall again cause a notice of its assessment to be published and delivered, or posted, as is required in making an assessment in the first instance; and the same proceedings may be taken until the Board shall finally determine that said assessment is just and correct.

SEC. 12. If the owner of any lot affected by said assessment is dissatisfied with the final action of the Board as to said assessment, he may appeal to the Supervisors at any time within five days after such final action, by filing with the Secretary of the Board of Public Works a notice of such appeal, and thereupon said Secretary shall, within two days after receiving notice of said appeal, transmit said assessment and diagram with said objections and notice of appeal to the Supervisors, and the said Supervisors shall, at their next regular meeting, not less than ten days from the receipt thereof, consider and determine the sufficiency of said objections. If they shall determine that said objections are well taken, they shall direct the Board of Public Works to modify or change said assessment in the particulars wherein it is erroneous, and thereupon the like proceedings shall be had in making the assessment as in the first instance. If the Supervisors shall determine that the objections to the assessment are not well taken, the Clerk of said Supervisors shall certify such determination upon said assessment, and return said assessment so certified to the Board of Public Works, and thereupon said assessment shall become final and conconclusive. When said assessment shall have so become final and conclusive, it, together with the diagram of the lots assessed, shall be recorded in a Book of Assessments, to be kept in the office of the Board of Public Works for that purpose, and the record thereof shall thereupon be signed by the President and Secretary of said Board, and thereafter the assessment shall be a lien upon the respective lots assessed until the same is cancelled or discharged as provided in this Article.

SEC. 13. The expenses incurred for any work authorized by this Chapter, except for such portion of any street as is required by law to be kept in order or repair by any person, company or corporation having railroad tracks thereon, shall be assessed upon the lots and lands fronting thereon, except as herein otherwise specially provided; each lot or portion of a lot being separately assessed, in proportion to its frontage, at a rate per front foot sufficient to cover the total expense of the work.

Subdivision One—The expense of work done on main street crossings, where the streets intersect each other at right angles, shall be assessed on the four quarter blocks adjoining and cornering upon the crossing, and each lot or part of lot in such quarter blocks fronting on such main street shall be separately assessed according to its proportion of frontage on the said main street.

Subdivision Two—The expense of work done on street intersections or crossings, when such intersections or crossings are not at right angles, shall be assessed upon an assessment district adjacent to such intersection or crossing, to be determined by the Board of Public Works, and delineated upon a map as aforesaid. Said assessment district shall not cover, on any street, more than one-half of the distance to any other main street crossing or intersection.

Subdivision Three—Where a main street terminates at a right angle in another main street, the expense of the work done on one-half of the width of the street opposite the termination shall be assessed upon the lots in each of the two quarter blocks adjoining and cornering on the same, according to the frontage of such lots on said main streets, and the expense of the work done on the other half of the width of said street, upon the lot or lots fronting such termination.

Subdivision Four—Where any small or subdivision street crosses a main street at right angles, the expense of all work done on said crossing shall be assessed on all the lots or portions of lots half way on said small streets to the next crossing or intersection, or to the end of such small or subdivision street, if it does not meet another.

Subdivision Five—The expense of work done on small or subdivision street crossings when such streets intersect each other at right angles, shall be assessed upon the lots fronting upon such small streets, on each side thereof in all directions half way to the next street or either side, respectively, or to the end of such street, if it does not meet another.

Subdivision Six—Where a small or subdivision street terminates at right angles in another street, the expense of the work done on one-half of the width of such street opposite the termination, shall be assessed upon the lots fronting on such small street so terminating according to their frontage thereon, half way on each side respectively, to the next street, or to the end of such street, if it does not meet another; and the expense of the work done on the other one-half of the width of said street upon the lot or lots fronting such termination.

Subdivision Seven—The expense of all other work, not herein specifically provided for, shall be assessed according to such rules and regulations as the Board of Public Works may have prescribed prior to the recommendation of said work.

Subdivision Eight—The owner of any lot or lands fronting upon any street, the width and grade of which have been legally established, may, at his own expense (after obtaining from the Board of Public Works permission so to do before said Board has passed its resolution of intention for grading said street), perform any grading upon said street to at least the center line thereof, to its grade as then established, and thereupon procure, at his own expense, a certificate from the City Engineer, setting forth the number of cubic yards of cutting and filling made by him in said grading, and that the same is done to the established grade of said street, and thereafter file said certificate with said Board, which certificate the Board shall record in a book kept for that purpose and properly indexed. When thereafter the Supervisors order the grading of said street, or any portion thereof, on which any grading, certificated as aforesaid, has been done, the said owner and his successors in interest shall be entitled to credit on the assessment upon his lots and lands fronting on said street for the grading thereof, to the amount of the cubic yards of cutting and filling set forth in his said certificate, at the prices named in the contract for said cutting and filling; or if the grade has meanwhile been changed, for so much of said certificated work as would be required for grading to the grade as changed. The Board shall include in the assessment for the whole of said grading the number of cubic yards of cutting and filling set forth in any and all certificates so recorded in its office, or if said grade has been changed, so much of said certificated work as would be required for grading thereto, and shall enter corresponding credits, deducting the same as payments made upon the amounts assessed against the lots and lands owned respectively by said certificated owner and his successors in interest.

Sec. 14. In making an assessment the Commissioners of Public Works shall act as a Board, and the assessment shall be authenticated by the signatures of all of said Commissioners as "Commissioners of the Board of Public Works;" and every assessment so authenticated and recorded in the Book of Assessments shall be *prima facie* evidence of the correctness and regularity of all proceedings of said Board and of the Supervisors prior to the date of such record.

Sec. 15. Upon the recording of an assessment as aforesaid, the President and Secretary of the Board of Public Works shall sign a warrant for its collection, and thereupon said assessment and diagram, with the warrant attached thereto, shall be delivered to the Tax Collector of said city and county for collection, who shall immediately give notice thereof by publication for ten days. Said notice shall set forth in general terms the locality and character of the work or improvement for which the assessment was made, and shall notify all persons interested that a warrant for its collection has been given to said Tax Collector, and that unless payment is made within thirty days from the first publication of said notice the property so assessed will be sold to satisfy said assessment.

Sec. 16. When the assessment upon any of the lots delineated on said diagram shall be paid, the Tax Collector shall write the word "Paid," together with the date of payment, opposite the number of said lot upon the assessment, and shall give to the person paying the same a receipt therefor, showing upon which lot said payment was made. Upon presentation of said receipt to the Secretary of the Board of Public Works, he shall immediately enter upon the record of such assessment the fact and date of such payment.

Sec. 17. After the expiration of thirty days from the first publication of said notice, the assessment therein named shall be delinquent, and within twenty days thereafter, the Tax Collector shall, after having published a notice for ten days, sell the lands upon which said assessments are delinquent. He shall add to the amount of the assessment on each lot its aliquot portion of the cost of advertising said sale. After making said sales the Tax Collector shall return the assessment and warrant, with a report of his doings indorsed thereon, to the office of the Board of Public Works, and the Secretary of said Board shall forthwith note in the record of said assessment, and opposite to the number of each lot sold, the fact of payment or of the sale of said lot by the Tax Collector, together with the date and the name of the purchaser.

Said report of the Tax Collector shall be *prima facie* evidence of the correctness of all the proceedings taken by him in the matter of collecting said assessment.

SEC. 18. The General Revenue Laws of the State in force at the time of said sale in reference to the manner and place of sale of property for delinquent taxes, the execution of certificates of sale and deeds therefor, the force and effect of such certificates and deeds, and the provisions of said laws in relation to the redemption from tax sales, except as herein otherwise provided, shall be applicable to the proceedings for the sale of land for delinquent assessments.

SEC. 19. If, at said sale, no person shall bid the amount of said assessment with the aforesaid cost, the Tax Collector shall bid in the said lot for the amount of the assessment and cost in the name of the City and County of San Francisco, and upon his filing a certificate of said sale with the Treasurer, the Treasurer shall transfer the amount so bid to the Street Department Fund, and shall forthwith notify in writing the Auditor of such transfer.

All moneys received by the Tax Collector in payment of any of said assessments, shall be by him paid to the Treasurer, who shall place the same to the credit of the Street Department Fund.

SEC. 20. When said sale is completed, the contractor shall present his demand for the work done under his contract to the Board of Public Works, which shall act upon the same. If said Board approve said demand or any part thereof, the same must then be presented to the Supervisors and audited by the Auditor, and when so audited shall be paid by the Treasurer out of the Street Department Fund.

SEC. 21.   The Board of Public Works may at any time, without any application therefor, recommend to the Supervisors to order the planking, paving or macadamizing of the portion of any street required by law to be planked, paved or macadamized by the person, company or corporation having railroad tracks thereon. Upon such recommendation the Supervisors may by ordinance order said work to be done, and direct said Board to notify said person, company, or corporation of the fact of the passage of such ordinance.   The Secretary of said Board shall thereupon forthwith in writing notify said person, company or corporation of the passage of said ordinance; and if said person, company or corporation shall not, within ten days after receiving said notice, commence in good faith to do said work and prosecute the same diligently to completion, said Board of Public Works shall invite sealed proposals for doing said work in the manner provided in this Article; and all of the provisions of this Article in regard to such proposals, to the awarding of contracts, to the execution of contracts, and to the doing of public work, shall apply to all similar proceedings taken under this section.   On the completion of the work to the satisfaction of said Board, the contractor shall be entitled to recover from such person, company or corporation the contract price for the cost and expense of said work, together with incidental expenses, in an action instituted in a court of competent jurisdiction.   On the trial of such action, the certificate of said Board of the completion of said work to its satisfaction shall be *prima facie* evidence of the regularity of all proceedings prior thereto and of plaintiff's right to recover in said action.

SEC. 22.   No ordinance for the improvement of any street, other than for sewers, sidewalks and curbs, except for the improvement of the streets constituting or lying along the water front of said city and county, and except for such work as is provided for in the next preceding section, shall be passed by the Supervisors without extending said improvement throughout the whole width of such street.

SEC. 23.   Wherever in this article the word "street" occurs, it shall be held to include all streets, lanes, alleys, places, courts, boulevards and avenues which have been, or may be hereafter, dedicated and open to public use, and whose grade and width have been legally established; and whose grade of all intermediate or intersecting streets in any one block shall be deemed to conform to the grades as established at the crossings of the main streets.

The word "improvement" shall be held to include grading, paving, planking, macadamizing, piling and capping; and the construction and repair of sewers, cess-pools, manholes, culverts, drains, sidewalks and curbs.

The term "main street" shall mean such street or streets as bound a block, and the term "street" shall include crossing.

The word "block" shall mean the blocks known or designated as such upon the maps and books of the Assessor.

The word "paved" shall include any pavement of stone, iron, wood or other material which the Supervisors may, by ordinance, order to be used; but no patented pavement shall be ordered during the existence of the patent therefor, until the owner of such patent shall have transferred to said city and county all right to the use of the same within said city and county, with the privilege to any person to manufacture and lay the same upon its streets, under any contract that may be awarded to him, or entered into by him, with said city and county.

The term "expense" shall include the price at which the contract was awarded, and the term "incidental expenses" shall include all expenses incurred in printing and advertising the work contracted for.

All notices and resolutions required in this Article to be published shall be published daily, legal holidays excepted, in the official newspaper.

All notices herein required to be served, whether by delivery, mailing or posting, may be so served by any male citizen of the age of twenty-one years, and his affidavit thereof shall be *prima facie* evidence of such service. The affidavit by the publisher of the official newspaper, or his clerk, of the publication of any notice required in this Article to be published shall be *prima facie* evidence of such publication.

Sec. 24. When the owners of all the lands, fronting upon any street, which is less than forty feet in width, for the entire distance of said street, or for the distance of one or more entire blocks, shall petition the Board of Public Works that the said 'street, or that portion thereof upon which said lands front, be closed, said Board may pass a resolution recommending that the same be closed. Before passing such resolution the Board shall cause a notice of the application to be published, and fix a time and place at which it will consider the same, and hear objections thereto, and upon such hearing shall determine whether it will recommend that the same be closed; and if it shall so determine, it shall transmit such recommendation to the Supervisors, and thereupon the Supervisors may pass an ordinance that the said street be closed; and the said street shall, upon the passage of said ordinance, be, and be deemed to be, closed, and shall not thereafter be, or be deemed to be, a public street, or subject to any public expense or improvement; and the land theretofore included within the roadway and sidewalks of said street shall thereafter be the property of said city and county. No such ordinance shall be passed until the said petitioners shall have paid all the expenses of said proceedings.

Sec. 25. In all cases where lands in said city and county shall be hereafter sub-divided and laid out into blocks or plats, sub-lots, streets and alleys, or when new streets or public grounds shall be laid out, opened, donated or granted to the public by any proprietor, the map or plat thereof shall be submitted to the Board of Public Works for its approval, and if the Board approve the same, such approval shall be by it indorsed upon the said map or plat, and said map with said approval shall then be filed in the office of the City and County Recorder; and without such approval indorsed thereon no such map or plat shall be filed in the office of said Recorder, or have any validity; nor shall any street, alley, or public ground hereafter opened and dedicated as such, become or be a public street or be subject to any public improvement or expense without such approval, indorsement and record. No street hereafter laid out shall be approved or become a public street unless the same shall be at least forty feet in width and two hundred feet distant from any parallel street, except it shall be the extension of a street already in existence.

SEC. 26. Said Board shall cause the principal streets to be sprinkled; and shall cause streets to be swept by hand labor, if said Board deem it best. If the work is done by contract, then said Board shall invite proposals for cleaning such of the streets of said city and county as said Board shall determine. Before causing notice for such proposals to be published said Board shall divide the city and county into such number of districts as in its judgment will best promote competition for bids, and secure the cleaning of the streets at the lowest cost. The Secretary of said Board shall, under its direction, on the first Monday in May of each year, cause to be published for a period of ten days, a notice inviting proposals for cleaning each of the aforesaid districts, specifying in said notice the streets of each district which are to be cleaned, the number of times a week that they are to be cleaned, and the amount of security to be given with each contract. Bids shall be made for each district separately. All the provisions of this Article in relation to the making and opening of bids, awarding of contracts and entering into and performance of contracts, shall be applicable to the contracts provided for in this section.

Said Board may also purchase one or more machines for sweeping the streets, and may cause the streets to be swept with said machines; and the Board of Public Works may cause all street sweepings to be delivered at a place or places designated by the Park Commisisoners.

The Board of Public Works may also order the streets swept by hand, preference being given to men of families; *provided*, persons thus employed shall have been residents of the city of San Francisco for six months preceding the date of their employment. Said Board may order all construction and repairs of streets, sewers and other municipal work performed by day laborers under its direction and supervision, whenever it may be required by the exigencies of the municipal government; said laborers shall be employed under the restrictions mentioned in this section.

SEC. 27. Said Board shall cause to be made all urgent repairs upon the public streets that may from time to time be requisite for the public safety, and for that purpose may employ such laborers as may be necessary, and at such wages as may be from time to time fixed by the Board, by and with the consent of the Mayor; but when the cost and expense of the repairs upon any street or portion of a street shall exceed the sum of five hundred dollars, exclusive of materials to be furnished from the Corporation Store Yard, the same shall be done under contract awarded in the manner provided in this Article.

Sec. 28. Said Board shall, from time to time, after it shall have been directed so to do by the Supervisors by ordinance, invite proposals for supplying to said city and county such materials as may be required for the repair of the public streets or for any improvement thereof, and such proceedings shall be had in awarding the contracts therefor, as are in this Article provided for awarding other contracts.

Sec. 29. The Supervisors shall select some place in said city and county, which shall be known as the Corporation Store Yard, wherein shall be kept all supplies, material, implements and machines belonging to said City and County, to be used in repairing or cleaning the streets or for any improvement thereon. Said Board of Public Works shall appoint a Storekeeper for said Corporation Store Yard, who shall hold his office during its pleasure. He shall have the custody of the Corporation Store Yard, and of all the supplies, materials and implements therein, and shall keep books of account in which shall be kept a systematic account of all purchases, and of the receipt of supplies and materials under any contracts awarded under the provisions of the preceding section, and of the delivery thereof, which books shall at all times show the amount of said materials and supplies on hand and in store, and when, to whom, and for what purpose each article was delivered. He shall be responsible for all materials and supplies placed in said Store Yard, and shall not deliver any article except upon the written order or requisition of the President and Secretary of the Board of Public Works, and he shall take the written receipt, indorsed upon said order, of each person to whom any delivery is made, specifying the date of such delivery and the amount and kind of material and supplies delivered. For any deficiency in his accounts or for the delivery of any article without such order or requisition and receipt, he shall be liable upon his official bond. All cobble stones, or stone blocks or other material with which any street or portion of a street may have been paved or planked shall, if at any time removed from said street, be taken to said Corporation Store Yard, and there kept, accounted for and disposed of by the Storekeeper in the same manner as other supplies.

CHAPTER III.

OF THE OPENING OF NEW STREETS.

SECTION 1. When an application shall be made to the Board of Public Works for the straightening, widening or extending of any street, or for the laying out, establishing or opening of a new street, signed by the owners of a majority of the frontage of the lands upon the line of said street, or proposed street, and such improvement requires the condemnation of private property, and the Board shall by resolution determine that the improvement would be of public benefit, it shall make an estimate of the cost and expense of such improvement, and determine by resolution the district which will be affected by, and should be assessed for, the cost and expense of such improvement. No proceedings shall be had upon the filing of such petition until after the persons signing the same shall have deposited with the Secretary of the Board an amount of money which, as may be determined by said Board, will be sufficient to defray all the cost and expense that may be incurred in case the Supervisors shall not pass an ordinance for said improvement.

SEC. 2. If within three months after the passage of the resolution determining such district, a majority of the owners of the land within said district who shall also be the owners of two-thirds of the superficial square feet of the property included within said district, and of three-fourths in value of said property—including improvements thereon—estimating said value according to the last preceding Assessment Book of said city and county, shall present to said Board a petition for said improvement, verified by their oaths and describing the lands of which they are the owners, and showing the amount at which the same was assessed upon the last preceding Assessment Book of said city and county, and stating that they are the owners and in possession of the lands named in said petition, the said Board shall pass a resolution of its intention to recommend said improvement to the Supervisors, and shall in such resolution specify a day upon which it will hear any objections that may be made to said improvement.

Before passing such resolution of intention, said Board shall cause to be prepared a map or diagram of the district affected by and to be assessed for the cost and expense of said improvement, upon which shall be delineated the several lots of land upon which said assessment is to be levied, and also the lots of land which are to be taken for said improvement, and showing the name of the person or persons to whom the said lots were assessed upon the last Assessment Book of said city and county, together with the amounts of such assessments.

SEC. 3. The Secretary of said Board shall thereupon cause said resolution of intention to be published for a period of thirty days, non-judicial days excepted, and shall also cause a copy of said resolution to be deposited, postage prepaid, in the post office at said city and county, addressed to each person whose name is delineated upon said map, at least ten days before the day named for hearing objections thereto.

SEC. 4. At any time before the day fixed in such resolution for hearing objections to said improvement, any person interested therein may file with the Secretary of said Board his objections thereto, briefly stating the grounds thereof and the nature of his interest; and upon the day fixed for hearing the same, or some day to which the hearing thereof shall then be postponed, said Board shall proceed to hear and determine the sufficiency of any objections which may have been filed.

SEC. 5. If said Board shall determine that such objections are sufficient to prevent a recommendation of the improvement, it shall pass a resolution to that effect, and no further proceedings shall be had under said petition. If no objections have been filed, or if the Board shall determine that the objections filed are insufficient, it may pass a resolution recommending to the Supervisors said improvement, and in its recommendation shall specially report to the Supervisors whether in its opinion the land within the district specified as affected by said improvement will be benefited to the extent of the cost and expense of said improvement.

SEC. 6. If said Board shall pass a resolution recommending said improvement, the Secretary shall forthwith transmit to the Clerk of the Supervisors a copy of said resolution, together with the petition, map, estimate of the cost and expense of said improvement, and any objections that may have been filed; and the Supervisors shall at their first regular meeting thereafter, or at such session, to which said hearing may be adjourned, pass upon said recommendation, and may, by resolution, adopt or reject the same. If said recommendation is rejected, no further action shall be had thereon or upon said petition. If the Supervisors shall adopt said recommendation, they shall within thirty days thereafter pass an ordinance providing for said improvement, and may in said ordinance prescribe such rules for the conduct of the Board of Public Works, respecting the assessment and valuation to be made by said Board, and providing for the condemnation of said lands, and the collection of said assessment, in addition to, and not inconsistent with, the rules herein prescribed, as to said Supervisors shall seem expedient. Upon the passage of said ordinance, the Clerk of the Supervisors shall transmit a certified copy thereof to the Board of Public Works.

SEC. 7. Upon the receipt by said Board of a certified copy of said ordinance, it shall cause to be made an accurate survey of the contemplated improvement, and a map thereof, upon which shall be delineated each and every lot of land to be taken or appropriated for the purposes of the intended improvement, showing its extent in feet and inches, and also each and every lot of land within the district determined to be affected by, and which is to be assessed for, the cost and expense of said improvement. After said survey and map are made, the Board shall pass a resolution fixing a day on or after which it will proceed to value the several lots of land to be taken for the purpose of the intended improvement, and ascertain and determine the damages and benefits which may result therefrom.

The Secretary of the Board shall cause said resolution

to be published for a period of ten days before the day fixed in said resolution for proceeding to make said valuation.

In estimating the damage to any lot by reason of any portion of said lot having been taken for public use, as herein provided, the measure of damage to said lot shall be the difference at the time of said appropriation between the value of said lot in its entirety and its value as reduced in size by the appropriation of a part thereof to said public use.

The cost and expense of the improvement shall include the value of the land taken, with the improvements, if any, thereon, and the expense of the proceedings for its appropriation or condemnation.

Sec. 8. On the day named in said notice and upon such other days as the matter may be continued to, from time to time, said Board shall proceed to value the several parcels of land necessary to be taken for the purpose of the intended improvement. The said value shall be ascertained as of the time of said inquiry, independently of any appreciation or depreciation that may be caused to the same by reason of such intended improvement, and the Board shall fix said valuation as the amount to be given to the owners therefor. The Board shall also assess the benefits and damages which may result from the contemplated improvement to the lands within said district, and shall distribute the total value of all the lands and improvements taken, together with the damages, if any caused by said improvement to the adjacent lands, and the estimated cost and expense of said improvement, in the form of an assessment upon each and every lot of land within the district determined to be affected by said improvement in proportion to the benefits which said Board shall determine will be received by said lots and lands.

Sec. 9. Before proceeding to make such valuation and assessment, the Commissioners of the Board of Public Works shall each take and subscribe an oath before one of the Judges of the Superior Court of said city and county that he has no interest in any of the land to be taken or assessed for the proposed improvement. The meetings of the Board, when engaged in making said valuation and assessment, shall be public, and held at the office of the Board, and all persons interested in any such valuation and assessment shall have the right to be present and be heard in person or by counsel. All persons claiming any interest in the lands to be taken for said improvement, or that will be damaged thereby, are required at or during such hearing, to file with the Board, plats, and a description of their respective lots of land.

SEC. 10. In making said assessment and valuation the Commissioners shall act as a Board, and said assessment and valuation shall be authenticated by the signatures of said Commissioners as "Commissioners of the Board of Public Works;" and every assessment and valuation so authenticated and recorded in the Book of Assessments for Condemnation shall be *prima facie* evidence of the correctness and regularity of all the proceedings of said Board and of the Supervisors prior to the date of such record.

SEC. 11. In determining the valuation of the property which is taken for said improvement, the Board shall, in its report, set forth, under appropriate headings, a brief description of each lot thereof, the amount allowed for the same, the name of the owner of each lot, when known (and if unknown, that fact shall be stated), and the name of any claimant thereto, or to any interest therein; and in making the assessment for the cost and expense of said improvement, the Board shall set forth in the assessment, under appropriate headings, a brief description of each lot assessed, the amount assessed against the same, the person to whom said property was assessed upon the next preceding Assessment Book of said city and county, the owner thereof, if known (and if unknown, that fact shall be stated), and the total amount of the cost and expense of said improvement.

SEC. 12. Upon the completion of said valuation and assessment, the Board shall cause to be published for ten days a notice of the completion of said assessment and valuation, notifying all parties interested therein to examine the same ; and for that purpose said assessment, valuation and maps shall be open and exhibited to public inspection at the office of the Board for thirty days after the first publication of said notice. During said period of thirty days, but not thereafter, the Board may alter, change or modify said assessment in any respect.

Upon the expiration of said thirty days, it shall complete the same in the form of a report and schedule, embracing the value of the lands taken and the assessment of said value, together with the cost and expense of the improvement, as hereinbefore provided, upon the several lots of land embraced within the aforesaid district. Said report and schedule shall, within sixty days after the first publication of the last mentioned notice, be filed in the office of the County Clerk, together with a petition signed by the President of said Board, to the Superior Court, praying for a judgment of said Court confirming the assessment contained therein against the respective lots therein described as assessed, and for the condemnation and conveyance to said city and county, upon the payment of the value thereof, as ascertained by said report, of each of the lots of land alleged in said petition to be necessary to be taken for said improvement.

SEC. 13. On filing such petition, and upon application to said Court, the Presiding Judge thereof shall appoint some day, not less than ten nor more than thirty days thereafter, as the time when any objections to the confirmation of said report will be heard by said Court. The Clerk of said Court shall thereupon cause to be published for ten days, in three daily papers in general circulation published in said city and county, one of which shall be the official newspaper, and the others of which shall be designated by said Judge, a notice of the filing of said report and of the day assigned for the hearing of any objections that may be made thereto. Any party interested therein may at any time before the day assigned for the hearing thereof, file in said Court his objections in writing, to the confirmation of the same, specifying his objections; and all objections not specified shall be deemed waived. Upon the the day fixed in said order, said Court shall proceed to the hearing of any objections that may have been filed to the confirmation of said report. Upon proof of publication of said notice said Court shall have and take jurisdiction of said report, and of the subject matter thereof, as a special proceeding, and upon said day, and at any other time or times to which said hearing may be adjourned, may hear the allegations of the parties and proofs adduced in support of the same, and may confirm said report, or change, alter or modify the same, or cause the same to be changed, altered or modified by said Board. Said judgment of confirmation shall be a lien upon each lot of land described in such report for the amount assessed against the same, and shall provide for the conveyance to said city and county of each and every of the lots of land declared necessary for the purpose of said improvement, upon the payment of the value thereof as fixed by such judgment.

SEC. 14. ˙Any person who has filed objections to the confirmation of said report may appeal from said judgment to the Supreme Court at any time within thirty days after the entry of such judgment. The amount of the undertaking on such appeal shall be fixed by said Presiding Judge, and such undertaking shall be made payable to the City and County of San Francisco. For the purposes of such appeal, the judgment roll of the proceedings in the Superior Court shall consist of the report, objections, judgment and bill of exceptions, or so much thereof as may be necessary to determine such appeal, and said appeal shall be heard by said Supreme Court on questions of law only. If said judgment be reversed or modified, the Superior Court shall take such proceedings as will cause said assessment and valuation to be made in accordance with the opinion of the Supreme Court. The City Attorney shall act as the attorney for the Board of Public Works in proceedings under this Chapter.

SEC. 15. After the confirmation of said report, if the time for appealing has expired or if an appeal has been taken and the judgment appealed from has been affirmed, upon the application of the Board of Public Works the Clerk of the Superior Court shall issue a certificate to that effect to said Board; and said assessment shall then be recorded in the Book of Assessments for Condemnation kept for that purpose, and the record thereof signed by the President and Secretary of said Board; and the Secretary shall then deliver to the Tax Collector the assessment so confirmed and recorded, together with said certificate of said Clerk, and a warrant to the Tax Collector directing him to collect the said assessment; and thereupon such proceedings shall be had in the collection of said assessment as are hereinbefore provided for the collection of assessments upon property for the improvement of streets.

Sec. 16. Upon the report of the Tax Collector to the Supervisors that the amount of said assessment has been collected and paid into the Treasury, the Supervisors shall order to be paid out of the Treasury the sums fixed in said judgment as the compensation for the lands to be taken for said improvement; and upon the delivery to the Treasurer, by any person entitled to receive compensation for any lot of land so taken, of a conveyance of said lot of land to the city and county, approved by the City Attorney, and a certificate from said City Attorney that such person is entitled to the compensation for the lands described in said conveyance, the Treasurer shall pay to said person the amount awarded for said lot by said judgment of condemnation, after the demand therefor has been audited by the Auditor.

Sec. 17. If the owner of any of said lots or subdivisions neglects or refuses for ten days, to make and deliver such conveyance, or is unable by reason of incapacity to make a good and sufficient conveyance thereof to said city and county, or if the City Attorney shall certify that the title to any of said lots is in dispute or uncertain, or that there are conflicting claimants to the amount awarded as compensation therefor, or to any part thereof, a warrant upon the Treasury for the payment of the amount so awarded shall be by order of the Supervisors drawn by the President and Secretary of the Board of Public Works, and, together with a certificate of the Treasurer indorsed thereon that the said warrant has been registered by him and that there are funds in the Treasury set apart to pay the same, be deposited with the County Clerk, and thereupon, upon a petition to said Presiding Judge by the President of the said Board, setting forth said facts, said Judge shall issue an order *ex parte* directing the Sheriff to place said Board in the possession of the said land.

Sec. 18. At any time thereafter any claimant to said award, or any part thereof, may file his petition in said Superior Court against all parties in interest for an adjudication of all conflicting claims to the same, or for an order that the same be paid to him, and thereupon such proceedings shall be had thereon as may be agreeable to law and equity. Upon entry of final judgment in such proceeding the County Clerk shall, after said demand has been audited by the Auditor, collect the warrant and pay the proceeds to the person or persons named in said judgment as entitled thereto. It shall be provided in said judgment that before receiving the proceeds of said warrant, said party, or some one authorized in his behalf, shall make and execute to said city and county and deliver to the County Clerk a sufficient conveyance of said lot of land.

Sec. 19. Immediately after taking possession of the land required for said street, said Board shall report that fact to the Supervisors.

Sec. 20. If any member of said Board be interested in any of the land to be taken or assessed for such improvement, the Mayor shall appoint, for the purpose of making the said assessment and valuation only, some competent person to act as one of the Commissioners therefor, who shall possess the same qualifications as are provided for said Commissioners, and who before entering upon his duties shall take the oath of office required of said Commissioners, and enter into a bond for such amount as may be fixed by the Supervisors.

CHAPTER IV.

OF SEWERS AND DRAINAGE.

Section 1. The Board of Public Works shall devise a general system of drainage which shall embrace all matters relative to the thorough, systematic and effectual drainage of said city and county, and shall from time to time make to the Supervisors such recommendations upon the subject of sewerage and drainage as it may deem proper.

Sec. 2. Said Board shall prescribe the location, form and material to be used in the construction, reconstruction and repairing of all public sewers, manholes, sinks, drains, cesspools, and other appurtenances belonging to the drainage system, and of every private drain or sewer emptying into a public sewer, and determine the place and manner of the connection.

Sec. 3. Said Board shall recommend to the Supervisors rules and regulations concerning the public and private sewers and drains in said city and county, and upon recommendation of said Board, the Supervisors are authorized to pass an ordinance establishing the same and prescribing the penalties for any violation thereof.

SEC. 4. No person shall connect with, or open or penetrate any public sewer or drain without first obtaining a permit in writing from said Board, and complying with the rules and regulations of said Board in reference thereto.

SEC. 5. Said Board may also recommend to the Supervisors the construction of such canals, sewers, tunnels, ditches, drains, embankments, reservoirs, pumping works, machinery and other works necessary for the proper and effectual drainage of said city and county, together with plans for connecting the same with sewers and private drains already constructed or thereafter to be constructed.

SEC. 6. The Supervisors may, upon the recommendation of said Board, by ordinance passed by the affirmative vote of not less than nine members, authorize the purchase of any personal property or the acquisition by purchase or condemnation of any real estate which may be necessary for the construction of any sewer or the making of any improvement provided for in this chapter. The title to all real estate purchased shall be taken in the name of said city and county.

SEC. 7. Said Board may, with the like approval of the Supervisors, agree with the owners of any real estate, upon which it is deemed desirable to construct any sewer or other improvement relative to sewerage or drainage, upon the amount of damage to be paid to such owners for the purpose of such improvement and for the perpetual use of said real estate for such purpose.

SEC: 8. Said Board may, when authorized by ordinance passed by the affirmative vote of not less than nine members of the Board of Supervisors, construct such sewers, reservoirs and pumping works on lands and made lands fronting on the Bay of San Francisco, and controlled by the Board of State Harbor Commissioners, as may be necessary to carry out the general system of sewerage for said city and county.

SEC. 9. When, upon the recommendation of said Board of Public Works, the Supervisors shall determine upon any improvement for the purpose of sewerage and drainage which necessitates the acquisition or condemnation of private property, and said Board is unable to agree with the owner thereof upon the amount of compensation or damages to be paid therefor, or when such owner is in any way incapable of making any agreement in reference thereto; and in all cases in which said Board shall deem it most expedient, it shall, when authorized by the Supervisors expressed by ordinance, have the right to cause said property to be condemned, and to institute proceedings for the condemnation of such property, or for the ascertainment of such damages in the manner, so far as the same is applicable, which is provided in this Article for the condemnation of real estate when necessary for the opening of any new street.

Sec. 10. Said Board shall have power to dispose of the garbage in any manner which they may deem to be for the best interest of the city.

Chapter V.

OF THE NEW CITY HALL.

Section 1. The Board of Public Works shall, immediately upon its organization, take charge of the land bounded by Larkin street, McAllister street and Park avenue, and the improvements thereon, and as soon as practicable thereafter, proceed with the construction of the buildings and improvements on said land, known as the New City Hall.

Sec. 2. The Secretary of said Board shall keep a record of its proceedings respecting the construction of the New City Hall, and said record shall be kept distinct from the general records of said Board. Said Secretary shall keep an account of said construction, and an account of the receipts and disbursements; and shall keep an account with each contractor and employee for any work done or material furnished for said construction.

Sec. 3. Said Board shall, by resolution, fix a day in each week for its regular meeting for the purpose of transacting business for the New City Hall, on which all its transactions in reference thereto shall be had.

Sec. 4. Said Board may allow demands of the contractors, from time to time, as work progresses or materials are furnished, but until the contract is completed such demands allowed thereon shall not exceed seventy-five per centum of the value of the labor or material furnished, which said value shall be ascertained and determined by the certificate of the Architect and Superintendent, subject to the approval of said Board.

SEC. 5. When said New City Hall is completed, said Board shall render to the Supervisors a full and final account of its transactions in reference to said New City Hall, and thereupon the duties of said Board in reference to the construction of the said New City Hall shall cease.

CHAPTER VI.

OF THE PARK COMMISSIONERS.

SECTION 1. The lands designated upon the map of the Outside Lands of said city and county, made in pursuance of Order Number Eight Hundred, by the word "Park," to wit: extending from Stanyan street on the east to the Pacific Ocean, and known as Golden Gate Park; and also the land fronting on Haight street, designated upon said map by the word "Park," and known as "Buena Vista Park;" and also the lands designated upon said map by the word "Avenue," extending from Baker street westward until it crosses Stanyan street; and also that certain highway bounded on the west by the Pacific Ocean, and designated upon said map as "Great Highway;" also "Mountain Lake Park;" also "Seal Rocks," as ceded to the City of San Francisco by Act of Congress approved February 23, 1887, and all other parks, squares and public grounds, in said city and county, shall be under the exclusive control and management of a Board of three Commissioners, who shall be styled Park Commissioners.

SEC. 2. Said Commissioners shall be the successors in office of the Park Commissioners holding office at the time this Charter shall go into effect by virtue of appointment under the provisions of an Act of the Legislature of the State of California, approved March 14, 1889, and the Act amendatory thereof, approved March 24, 1893.

SEC. 3. Said Commissioners shall be appointed by the Mayor, and shall hold office for four years. Those first appointed under this Charter shall immediately upon their appointment so classify themselves by lot that the term of office of one of said Commissioners shall expire at the expiration of two years one at the expiration of three years, and one at the expiration of four years, from the date of their appointment.

SEC. 4. Said Commissioners shall organize as a Board by electing one of their number President, and may elect a Secretary who is not a member of the Board. The person so elected President shall hold his office for one year and until his successor is elected.

Said Commissioners shall receive no compensation. Two of said Commissioners shall constitute a quorum for the transaction of business, but no contract shall be entered into authorizing the expenditure of money without the approval of all of said Commissioners.

SEC. 5. Such Board of Park Commissioners shall have the full and exclusive power to govern, manage and direct the Parks, Avenues and grounds, which have been or shall be placed under its care and charge; to employ and appoint such Superintendents, Laborers, Clerks, or Secretaries, Attorney, Surveyors, Engineers; to engage and employ musicians for service in the Park, and other officers and assistants as to said Board shall seem necessary and expedient for the proper management of the said Parks and of its affairs; the said Park Commissioners shall also have power in their discretion, and when the interest of the Park will justify the same, to furnish for the ornamentation and planting of the school lots of the city such plants, trees, shrubbery, flowers, etc., as they may be able to spare from the Park nurseries; and to maintain a museum and accept of any articles therefor; to purchase and maintain such neat animals as in their discretion may be of interest to the public; also to prescribe and fix the duties, authority, and compensation of such appointees and employees, and to have the management and disbursements of all funds legally appropriated or provided for the support of said Park and grounds; *provided*, that no moneys shall for any of said purposes be paid out of the Treasury of said city and county, except upon warrants duly signed by a majority of the Board of Park Commissioners thereof, and duly audited by the Auditor of said city and county.

SEC. 6. To appoint and maintain out of the moneys entrusted to its management as many Park Police for said public grounds as it may deem requisite for the purpose of enforcing its ordinances and regulations, and to provide a place of detention within either of said public grounds in which the persons arrested for violating any of said ordinances or regulations may be detained temporarily, or until the Park Police can deliver the person arrested to the Municipal Police.

SEC. 7. To expend the moneys appropriated by the Supervisors, or received from any source, for the purpose of managing and improving said public grounds.

SEC. 8. Said Park Police shall have authority to arrest, and hold to such bail as in the ordinance or regulation may be fixed as the maximum penalty for the violation thereof, or as may be prescribed by regulation by said Park Commissioners, any person found in the act of violating any ordinance or regulation of said Park Commissioners or of said city and county.

SEC. 9. Said Board shall have exclusive control and disposition of the moneys provided for the management and improvement of said public grounds.

SEC. 10. No money shall be paid out of the Treasury for any salary or expenditure incurred in the management or improvement of said public grounds, unless the same shall have been previously allowed by at least two of said Commissioners, and such allowance be indorsed upon the face of the demand, and specify the purpose for which said expenditure was made.

SEC. 11. It shall be lawful for every such Board of Park Commissioners to pass and adopt such ordinances as they may deem necessary for the regulation, use and government of the parks and grounds under their supervision, not inconsistent with the laws of the State of California. Such ordinances shall, within five days after their passage, be published for ten days, Sundays excepted, in a daily newspaper published in the city or city and county in which such Board shall be acting, to be selected by the said Board. All persons violating or offending against any such ordinances shall be deemed guilty of a misdemeanor, and shall be punished therefor on conviction in any court of competent jurisdiction.

SEC. 12. Every such Board of Park Commissioners is authorized and empowered to accept and receive donations and aid from individuals and corporations, and legacies and bequests by the last wills of deceased persons, for the aid or improvement of the parks and grounds under the control of such Board; and all moneys that shall be derived by any such Board from such donations, legacies and bequests, shall, unless otherwise provided by the terms of such gift, legacy or bequest, be deposited in the Treasury of the city or city and county in which said parks and grounds shall be situated, and shall be withdrawn therefrom and paid out in the same manner as is provided for the payment of moneys legally appropriated for the support and improvements of such parks and grounds; provided, however, that if the moneys derived from such gifts, bequests or legacies shall at any time exceed in amount the sum necessary for immediate expenditures on said parks and grounds, or if, in the judgment of the said Board of Park Commissioners, it should be advisable to invest the same, or a part thereof, in some interest-bearing or productive investment, the said Board of Park Commissioners are hereby authorized to invest the said moneys or any part thereof in interest-bearing bonds of the Government of the United States, or of the State of California, and thereafter to sell and dispose of said bonds, or to change the form of said investment, as to said Board shall deem best.

SEC. 13. Every such Board of Park Commissioners shall annually and on the first Monday of July of each year make to the Board of Supervisors of the city and county a full report of the proceedings, and a detailed statement of its receipts and expenditures.

SEC. 14. No Board of Park Commissioners shall in any year incur any debt or liability nor expend any money beyond the amount of moneys legally applicable during such year to the support, preservation and improvement of the parks and grounds under the control of such Board.

The Board of Park Commissioners of the City and County of San Francisco shall have the power to lease to the State of California for the term of not less than fifty nor more than one hundred years, on such terms as said Board may deem proper, a plot of ground in the Golden Gate Park not more than seven hundred feet square, on which the State of California may erect and maintain an Exposition Building, in which may be exhibited the products of the several counties of the State, and in which the collections made by the Mining Bureau may be maintained and exhibited.

SECTION 15. The Board of Supervisors is hereby authorized and empowered to levy and collect each year, in the mode prescribed by law for the levy and collection of taxes, a tax of not less than six nor more than ten cents upon each one hundred dollars assessed valuation of taxable property within the City and County of San Francisco, for the purpose of preserving, maintaining and improving the parks and grounds under the control of the Board of Park Commissioners. All moneys collected and arising from the said tax shall be paid by the Tax Collector, or other officer collecting the same, into the Treasury of said city and county, and shall be deemed to be thereupon appropriated and set apart for the maintenance, preservation and improvement of said parks and grounds, and shall be paid out by the Treasurer upon warrants signed by a majority of the said Board of Park Commissioners, and audited by the Auditor of such city and county.

CHAPTER VII.

OF HARBORS AND WHARVES.

SECTION 1. All the wharves, water front and Harbor of San Francisco which now or may hereafter belong to said city and county, or over which it may at any time lawfully exercise jurisdiction and control, shall be under the management and control of the Supervisors. All said wharves shall be built and repaired by the Board of Public Works, after proceedings had as provided in this Article for the improvement or repair of public buildings.

SEC. 2. The Supervisors shall by ordinance fix and regulate the tolls for wharfage and dockage and other charges, except where the wharves are under the jurisdiction of the Board of State Harbor Commissioners, and shall provide for the collection of the same; or may provide that no charges, tolls, dockage or wharfage be imposed or collected. The Supervisors shall not have power to dispose of any wharf, but they may lease any wharf for a term not exceeding three years.

ARTICLE VII.

Public Schools and Libraries.

CHAPTER I.

OF THE BOARD OF EDUCATION.

SECTION 1. The School Department shall be under the control and management of a Board of Education, composed of five School Directors, who shall be appointed by the Mayor. They shall not be less than thirty years of age and must have been residents of said city and county for at least five years prior to such appointment. They shall receive no compensation. Said appointments shall be made without regard to politics, and by preference from heads of families, irrespective of sex; and the persons so appointed shall hold office for four years. Those first appointed shall immediately after their organization as a Board, so classify themselves by lot that two of their number shall go out of office at the expiration of one year, one at the expiration of two years, one at the expiration of three years, and one at the expiration of four years.

SEC. 2. Immediately after their appointment and qualification, they shall organize by electing one of their number President, who shall serve for one year and until his successor is elected; and shall elect a Secretary, who is not a member of the Board.

The Board of Education shall meet weekly, and at such other times as it may determine. It shall determine the rules of its proceedings, but the concurrent vote of three members shall be necessary to transact business, and the ayes and noes shall be taken when demanded by any member, and entered on the records of the Board.

SEC. 3. All sessions shall be public, but executive sessions may be held by unanimous vote, and the records of the proceedings of the Board shall be open to public inspection.

SEC. 4. The Secretary of the Board of Education shall have power to administer oaths and affirmations concerning any demand upon the Treasury and in all other matters relating to his official duties.

Chapter II.

OF SCHOOLS.

Section 1. The School Department shall comprise all the public schools of the City and County of San Francisco, and shall include Primary and Grammar Schools, and may, at the option of the Board of Education, include Evening, Deportment, Technical, Scientific, Cosmopolitan, High and Normal Schools.

Sec. 2. Instruction must be furnished free of expense to all children residing in said city and county, in such branches as the Board of Education may determine; said instruction must include the branches necessary for a common school education, and may include the higher branches taught in the Grammar, High and Normal Schools of the said city and county.

Sec. 3. All children between the ages of six and twenty-one, residing within said City and County, are entitled to receive the benefits of a common school education, and may be instructed in ·such higher branches of education as may be established or provided by the Board of Education; but said Board shall not establish or maintain schools for instruction in the higher branches of education until full and ample facilities are provided for instruction in the Primary and Grammar classes of the public schools, in the order herein named. Adults shall be entitled to free instruction in the Evening Schools.

Sec. 4. Said Board may establish Kindergarten Schools for the tuition of children between the ages of four and six years, and may provide for Kindergarten instruction in the Primary Grades.

Sec. 5. Upon the establishment of Kindergarten Schools, the teachers thereof, as far as practicable, shall be chosen from the corps of teachers actually engaged in kindergarten instruction in this city at the time of such establishment.

Chapter III.

OF THE POWERS OF THE BOARD OF EDUCATION.

Section 1. The Board of Education shall have power:

1. To establish school districts, having regard to population and growth of the city and county, and to fix and alter the boundaries thereof.

2. To establish and maintain public schools as provided for in this Charter, and to change, modify, consolidate or discontinue the same as the public good may require.

3. To employ, pay and dismiss such teachers and persons as may be necessary to carry into effect its powers and duties, and to fix, alter and approve their salaries and compensation; to withhold for good and sufficient cause, the whole or any part of the wages, salaries or compensation of any person or persons employed as aforesaid; but no teacher shall be dismissed, except for sufficient cause which shall be determined by said Board after giving the accused teacher due hearing in his or her defense. Nothing herein contained shall curtail the right of the Board to engage teachers under special contracts or to establish rules for their appointment. No permanent appointment shall be made until after six months' probation in actual teaching in the Public Schools in this city and county.

4. The Board of Education shall not appoint any person to be a teacher in the primary or grammar classes of the schools of this city and county except upon competitive examination of those persons holding teachers' certificates, and who have been educated in the public school system of the State of California.

5. To grant and to revoke teachers' certificates.

6. To establish and enforce all necessary rules and regulations for the government and efficiency of the schools, and for carrying into effect the school system; to prevent and remedy truancy, and to reform truants; to compel the attendance at school of children between the ages of six and fourteen, without lawful occupation, found wandering about the streets or in public places during school hours.

7. To investigate charges against any person connected with or in the employ of the School Department; to administer oaths and take testimony in the conduct of such investigations; and to require the attendance of witnesses before the Board or any member or committee thereof. Any person summoned and refusing to attend and testify shall be deemed guilty of a misdemeanor and any person testifying falsely shall be deemed guilty of perjury.

8. To adopt or reject text books for the use of the schools; but such text books shall not be changed or modified within a period of four years after their adoption.

9. To provide for the School Department all supplies and material necessary for use in the schools, or in the offices of the Board or Superintendent, in the manner hereinafter provided; and to incur incidental expenses not exceeding two hundred dollars a month. All such materials and supplies shall be of California manufacture; *provided*, the cost shall not exceed the cost of imported articles.

10. To rent buildings or rooms for school purposes and furnish them with proper school furniture, apparatus and school appliances; to use and control such buildings as may be necessary for the requirements of the Department, and to insure such School property as may be deemed advisable.

11. To take possession of, receive, purchase, lease, and hold in fee, in trust for the City and County of San Francisco, any and all real estate, and all personal property, that has been or which hereafter may be acquired for the use and benefit of the schools of said city and county.

12. On or before the first day of April in each year to appoint School Census Marshals, and notify the Superintendent of Common Schools of such appointment.

13. To sue, in the name of the Board of Education, for any and all lots, lands and property belonging to or claimed by the School Department of said city and County, and to prosecute and defend all actions at law or special proceedings or suits in equity concerning the enjoyment and possession of said lots, lands and property; and to require the services of the City and County Attorney in all actions, suits and proceedings by or against said Board of Education.

14. To establish regulations for the disbursement of all moneys belonging to the School Department or to the Common School Fund, and to secure strict accountability in the expenditure thereof; to provide for the prompt payment, on not later than the tenth day of each month in every year, of all salaries due and allowed officers, teachers and other employees of the School Department; and for this purpose the Auditor shall

annually segregate so much of the Common School Fund as shall not exceed thirty dollars for each pupil in average daily attendance in the public schools of said city and county during the preceding fiscal year; and the amount so segregated shall not be applied to the payment of any demand against said Common School Fund during any fiscal year, other than for salaries, until all the salaries for that fiscal year have been fully paid or provided for. Said Board shall ascertain, determine and transmit to the Auditor, on or before the first day of July of each year, an estimate of the amount required for such segregation within said limit of thirty dollars.

15. To dispose of and sell such personal property used in the schools as shall no longer be required. All moneys realized by such sales shall be paid into the Treasury to the credit of the Common School Fund.

16. To lease for the benefit of the Common School Fund, for a term not exceeding twenty years, any real property of the School Department not required for school purposes; but no lease for a term exceeding two years shall be made, except by an affirmative vote of not less than four members of said Board, approved by an ordinance of the Supervisors, passed by the affirmative vote of not less than nine members.

17. To receive and manage property or money acquired by bequest or donation in trust for the benefit of any school, educational purpose, or school library; and to carry into effect the terms of any bequest not in conflict with then existing laws or this Charter.

18. To do and perform such acts as may be necessary and proper to carry into effect the powers conferred upon such Board.

SEC. 2. The Board of Education shall procure all supplies necessary for the public schools. All supplies, books, stationery, fuel, printing, goods, material, merchandise, and every other article supplied to or for the public schools, or any of them, when the expenditure to be incurred exceeds five hundred dollars, shall be furnished by contract let by said Board to the lowest responsible bidder, after advertisement for ten days.

SEC. 3. Said Board shall annually, on the first day of May, or within five days thereafter, make a list of supplies estimated to be required by the School Department for the ensuing fiscal year, stating in clear and explicit terms the quantities and kinds of all articles needed and how and when to be delivered, and shall invite proposals for furnishing the same, by advertising therefor for at least ten days in the official paper.

The provisions of sections 22, 23, 24, 25 and 26, of Chapter I, Article VI, of this Charter, in regard to the advertising for proposals, the form and character of proposals, the affidavit and security accompanying the same, the presentation and opening of proposals, the awarding and entering into of contracts and the security for the performance thereof, shall, so far as the same can be made applicable, apply to all proposals and contracts made, awarded or entered into for furnishing supplies to said Board of Education.

Any contract made in violation of any of said provisions shall be absolutely void, and never form the basis of, or be a claim against the Common School Fund or any other fund.

SEC. 4. Said Board shall, during each year, transmit to the Supervisors of said city and county, a report in writing for the preceding fiscal year, stating the number of schools within its jurisdiction; the length of the time they have been kept open; the number of pupils taught in each school; the daily average attendance of pupils in all the public schools; the number, names and salaries of teachers; the amount of money drawn from the Treasury by the Department during the year, distinguishing the State Funds from all others; from what sources, and the purposes for which such money has been expended, with particulars; and such other information as may be required from it by the State Superintendent, the Supervisors or the Mayor.

SEC. 5. Said Board shall, between the first and thirty-first days of May of each year, adopt a schedule of salaries for teachers and all other employees of the School Department, to take effect on the first day of July following.

CHAPTER IV.

OF THE SUPERINTENDENT OF SCHOOLS.

SECTION 1. The Superintendent of Schools of the City and County of San Francisco shall be *ex officio* a member of the Board of Education, without the right to vote.

SEC. 2. The Board of Education may appoint three Deputy Superintendents. When the daily average attendance in all the schools reaches 40,000, the Board of Education may appoint an additional Deputy Superintendent; and thereafter the said Board may appoint an additional Deputy Superintendent for each subsequent increase of 7,000 in daily average attendance.

SEC. 3. It shall be the duty of the Superintendent to recommend to the Board of Education the dismissal of teachers and the cancellation of their certificates, stating the reasons therefor.

SEC. 4. To observe and enforce all rules and regulations of the Board of Education, and to see that no religious or sectarian books or teachings are allowed in the schools, and to report quarterly to the Board.

SEC. 5. To report to the Board of Education annually, on or before the twentieth day of August, and at such other times as the Board of Education may require, all matters pertaining to the condition and progress of the public schools of said city and county, during the fiscal year, with such recommendation as he may deem proper.

SEC. 6. To attend all sessions of the Board of Education and inform said Board of the condition of the schools, school-houses, and other matters connected therewith; and to recommend such measures as he may deem necessary for the advancement of education in the city and county.

SEC. 7. To notify the Board of Education, at all times, of any waste, misappropriation, or useless expenditure connected with the School Department, that may come to his knowledge.

SEC. 8. To become acquainted with all the laws, rules and regulations governing the Public Schools in the city and county, and to give advice on subjects connected with the Public Schools gratuitously to officers, teachers, pupils and the parents and guardians of pupils.

SEC. 9. To cause the instruction in the Public Schools to be applied as far as possible to the practical affairs of life, to enable pupils to earn a living, and to cultivate a respect for truth, labor and industry.

SEC. 10. The Deputy Superintendents shall assist

the Superintendent, and perform such other duties as may be assigned them by the Superintendent and the Board of Education.

SEC. 11. The Superintendent and Deputy Superintendents shall meet at least semi-annually at such times as they may determine for the purpose of holding examinations for the granting of teachers' certificates, examine teachers and recommend to the Board of Education the granting of certificates.

SEC. 12. The Superintendent and Deputy Superintendents shall conduct the competitive examinations of teachers for the primary and grammar classes under the rules prescribed by the Board of Education; and shall report the results of such examinations to said Board.

CHAPTER V.

OF THE COMMON SCHOOL FUND.

SECTION. 1. The Common School Fund shall be used and applied by said Board of Education as follows, viz.:

1. For the prompt payment of the salaries or wages of the Superintendent, Deputy Superintendents, Teachers, Janitors, School Census Marshals, Secretary and other persons lawfully employed by said Board and in said School Department.

2. For supplying the Schools with fuel, water, apparatus, blanks, blank-books and necessary school appliances and also text books for indigent children.

3. For lighting and heating school rooms and the offices and rooms of said Board, and of the Superintendent.

4. For supplying books, printing and stationery for the use of said Board, the Superintendent, and for the incidental expenses of the Department.

5. For the purchase or rent of any real property or personal property purchased or hired by said Board.

6. For the construction, alteration, repairing and furnishing of school houses.

7. For grading, fencing and improving school lots.

8. For the discharge of incumbrances on any school property.

9. For the insurance of such school property as it may deem advisable to insure.

10. For the payment of interest accruing on school bonds; and for the redemption of the same, as far as the money in said Fund may be realized from the rents of property belonging to the School Department, dedicated to that purpose, or from money appropriated for such purpose by the State or city and county, and paid into such Fund.

Sec. 2. All demands payable out of the Common School Fund shall be filed with the Secretary of the Board of Education, and after they have been approved by the Finance Committee, and the Board of Education, upon an affirmative vote of three members thereof, upon the call of the ayes and noes (which shall be recorded), they shall be signed by the President of said Board, and the Superintendent, and sent to the Auditor. Every demand shall have endorsed upon it a certificate signed by the Secretary of its approval by the Board of Education, showing the date thereof, the vote thereon, and the law authorizing it, by title, date and section. Every person in the employ of the the School Department, entitled to a salary therefrom, shall receive a warrant for the amount due and approved by the Board, signed by the President and Secretary thereof; but the entire monthly salary roll of the Department shall be made up by the Secretary of said Board, and after being audited by the Finance Committee thereof, shall be presented at a regular meeting of said Board for its approval; and if approved by a majority of all the members thereof, upon a call of the ayes and noes (which shall be recorded), shall be endorsed in the same manner as other demands. The salary roll so audited, approved and indorsed, shall be immediately transmitted to the Auditor for comparison with the individual salary warrants issued in the manner above provided; but payment shall be made only on the individual warrants issued in accordance herewith.

Chapter VI.

OF THE SCHOOL TAX LEVY.

Section 1. The Board of Education shall, on or before the first Monday of May in each year, report to the Supervisors an estimate of the amount which shall be required during the ensuing fiscal year for the purpose of meeting the current annual expenses of public instruction in said city and county during said ensuing year, specifying the amount required for supplies to be furnished pupils, including text books; for purchasing and procuring sites; for leasing rooms or erecting buildings; for furnishing, fitting up, altering, enlarging and repairing buildings; for the support of schools organized since the last annual apportionment; for the salary of the Superintendent and all persons employed in the School Department, and for other expenditures necessary for the economical administration of the Public School system; but the aggregate amount so reported shall not exceed the sum of thirty-two and fifty one-hundredth dollars for each pupil who in the year ending December 31st, immediately prior thereto, has actually attended the schools entitled to participate in the apportionment. The average number of pupils attending the schools during any one year shall be ascertained by adding together the number of days' attendance of said pupils during the year, and dividing the same by the number of school days in the year.

SEC. 2 The Supervisors at the time and in the manner of levying and collecting other city and county taxes shall levy and cause to be collected for the Common School Fund a tax which shall produce an amount of money which, added to the revenue derived from other sources, shall not exceed thirty-two and fifty one-hundredth dollars for each pupil, as ascertained and reported by said Board.

SEC. 3. No school in which the religious doctrines or tenets of any particular religious sect are taught, inculcated or practiced, or in which any book containing compositions favorable or prejudicial to the doctrine or tenets of any particular religious sect is used, shall receive any portion of the school moneys ; nor shall any such book or teachings or practices be permitted in the public schools.

SEC. 4. Any member or officer of the Board of Education who shall, while in office, accept any donation or gratuity in money, or of any valuable thing, either directly or indirectly, from any teacher, or candidate, or applicant for position as teacher, upon any pretense whatever, shall be removed from office by the Board of Education and shall be guilty of a misdemeanor.

SEC. 5. Any member, officer or employee of the Board of Education, who shall accept any money or valuable thing, or the promise thereof, with an agreement or understanding, express or implied, that any person shall, in consideration thereof, receive the vote or influence of such member, officer or employee of any kind, in the School Department, for any purpose whatever, shall be removed from office by the Board of Education, and shall be guilty of a misdemeanor.

CHAPTER VII.

OF SCHOOL HOUSES AND LOTS.

SECTION 1. When a district in said city and county is unprovided with sufficient school accommodations, and suitable class rooms cannot be leased or rented at a reasonable price within said district, and more than two hundred pupils attend schools in such district which are sufficiently near to each other to be consolidated, the Board-of Education may, by resolution, make a requisition upon the Board of Public Works for plans and specifications and estimates for a new school house, specifying the number of class rooms needed, the location of the proposed school house, the date on which it should be completed, the amount of money in the School Fund available for the purpose, and such other information as will enable the Board of Public Works to prepare the necessary plans, specifications and estimates of cost for such school house.

If such plans, specifications and estimates are approved by the Board of Education, they shall be endorsed "Approved," with the date of such approval, by the President and Secretary thereof, and returned to the Board of Public Works, which shall proceed without delay to have said school house constructed and completed in accordance therewith.

When said school house is completed, the Board of Public Works shall notify the Board of Education, which thereupon shall examine the same, and if built in accordance with the plans and specifications approved by it, and within the estimated cost thereof, shall accept and take possession thereof. At least twenty-five per cent. of the contract price shall be retained until the expiration of thirty-five days after such acceptance.

9

Sec. 2. When any school house, building, or fence, belonging to, or connected with, or under the control of the Board of Education needs repairing, altering or improving, said Board shall notify the Board of Public Works, specifying in general terms the work to be done; and the Board of Public Works shall cause the same to be done forthwith, if the cost thereof shall not exceed two hundred and fifty dollars; otherwise, the Board of Public Works shall submit plans, specifications and estimates of cost to the Board of Education for its approval, and if approved as provided in Sec. 1 of this Chapter, the Board of Public Works shall cause the same to be done, and if done in accordance with the plans and specifications, and within said estimate, the same shall be accepted and paid for out of the Common School Fund.

Sec. 3. When it is necessary to purchase a lot for the use of the School Department, the price paid for such lot shall not exceed the market value of the adjacent property of equal size and similarly situated. Any school building constructed on such lot shall have a clear space of at least ten feet around the same.

Chapter VIII.

OF EMERGENCIES.

Section 1. In case of extreme emergency or great calamity, such as disaster from fire, riot, earthquake, or public enemy, the Board of Education may, with the approval of the Mayor and Supervisors, incur extraordinary expenditures in excess of the annual limit provided in this Charter, for the repair and construction and furnishing of school houses, in place of those so injured or destroyed; and the Supervisors may, by ordinance, cause to be transferred to the Common School Fund, from moneys in any fund not otherwise appropriated, sufficient money to liquidate such expenditures, and provide for the same in the next tax levy of said city and county.

Chapter IX.

OF THE PUBLIC LIBRARY AND READING ROOMS.

Section 1. The Public Library and Reading Rooms now existing in this city and county shall be under the management of a board of eleven trustees. The present

Board of Trustees of said Library and Reading Rooms shall have the management and control thereof until its successors are appointed as provided in this Chapter.

SEC. 2. The Mayor shall appoint eleven Trustees, who shall hold office for four years. Those first appointed shall so classify themselves by lot that three of their number shall go out of office in one year, three in two years, three in three years, and two in four years.

SEC. 3. The position of Trustee shall be one of honorary trust, without salary or compensation.

SEC. 4. The Supervisors shall, in making the annual tax levy, and as a part thereof, apportion the sum of two cents on the one hundred dollars for the purpose of maintaining said Library and Reading Rooms and such branches thereof as said Board may from time to time establish, and for purchasing books, journals and periodicals, and for purchasing or leasing real and personal property, and for constructing such buildings as may be necessary.

SEC. 5. All revenue from said tax, together with all money or property derived by gift, devise, bequest or otherwise, for the purposes of said Library, shall be paid into the Treasury, and be designated as the Library Fund, and be applied to the purposes herein authorized. If such payment into the Treasury would be inconsistent with the conditions or terms of any such gift, devise or bequest, said Board shall provide for the safety and preservation of the same and the application thereof to the use of said Library and Reading Room, in accordance with the terms and conditions of such gift, devise or bequest.

SEC. 6. The title to all property, real and personal now owned or hereafter acquired by purchase, gift, devise, bequest or otherwise, for the purpose of said Library and Reading Rooms, when not inconsistent with the terms of its acquisition, shall vest and be, and remain in said city and county, and in the name of said city and county may be sued for and defended by action at law or otherwise.

SEC. 7. Said Board shall take charge of said Public Library and Reading Rooms, and branches thereof, and of all real and personal property thereunto belonging, or that may be acquired by loan, purchase, gift, devise or otherwise, when not inconsistent with the terms and conditions of the gift, devise or bequest; it shall meet for business purposes on the first Tuesday of each month, and at such times as it may appoint, in a place to be provided for the purpose, and a majority shall constitute a quorum for the transaction of business. It shall elect one of its number President, who shall serve for one year and until his successor is elected, and shall elect a Librarian and such assistants as may be neccessary. It may elect a Secretary, who shall keep a full account of all property, money, receipts and expenditures, and a record of all its proceedings.

SEC. 8. Said Board, by a majority vote of all its members, to be recorded in its minutes with the ayes and noes, shall have power:

1. To make and enforce all rules, regulations and by-laws necessary for the administration, government and protection of said Library and Reading Rooms and branches thereof, and all property belonging thereto, or that may be loaned thereto.

2. To administer any trust declared or created for such Library and Reading Rooms and branches thereof, and provide memorial tablets and niches to perpetuate the memory of those persons who make valuable donations thereto.

3. To define the powers and prescribe the duties of all officers; determine the number of, and elect all necessary subordinate officers and assistants, and at its pleasure remove any officer or assistant.

4. To purchase necessary books, journals, publications and other personal property.

5. To order the drawing and payment upon vouchers, certified by the President and Secretary, of money from the Library Fund for any liability or authorized expenditure; and generally to do all that may be necessary to carry into effect the provisions of this Charter with reference to said Library and Reading Rooms and branches thereof.

6. To fix the salaries of the Librarian and Secretary and their assistants, and with the approval of the Supervisors, expressed by ordinance, to rent and equip such building or buildings, room or rooms, as may be necessary for said Library and Reading Rooms and branches thereof.

7. To establish such branches of said Library and Reading Rooms as the growth of the city may from time to time demand.

SEC. 9. Said Board on or before the first day of August, in each year, shall make a report to the Supervisors, giving the condition of its trust, with full statements of all property and money received, whence derived, how used and expended, the number of books, journals, and other publications on hand, the number added by purchase, gift or otherwise, during the next preceding fiscal year, the number lost or missing, the number and character of those loaned; and such other statistics, information and suggestions as may be of general interest; and also a financial report, showing all receipts and disbursements, with particulars thereof, and the names of all employees, and the salary paid to each.

SEC. 10. The Supervisors shall have power to appropriate and authorize the use, either in whole or in part, of any real estate belonging to said City and County, for the purpose of erecting and maintaining a building or buildings thereon, to be used for said Library and Reading Rooms, or branches thereof, and may appropriate the whole or any portion of any public building belonging to said City and County for such use.

SEC. 11. Said Board shall have such other powers and privileges not inconsistent with the provisions of this Charter as are set forth in an Act of the Legislature of this State entitled, "An Act to establish and maintain Free Public Libraries and Reading Rooms." Approved March 18th, 1878.

CHAPTER X.

OF THE SAN FRANCISCO LAW LIBRARY.

SECTION 1. The Supervisors are authorized and required by ordinance to provide, fit up and furnish, and provide with fuel, lights, stationery, and all necessary conveniences, attendants and care, rooms convenient and accessible to the Judges and officers of the Courts and of the municipal government of said city and county sufficient for the use and accommodation of the San Francisco Law Library, established under an Act of the Legislature of this State entitled: "An Act to provide for increasing the Law Library of the corporation known as the San Francisco Law Library, and to secure the use of the same to the Courts held at San Francisco, the Bar, the city and county government and the people of the City and County of San Francisco." Approved March 9th, 1870. The Supervisors are further authorized to appropriate, allow, and order paid out of the proper fund such sums as may be necessary for the purposes aforesaid; and all sums lawfully appropriated and expended pursuant hereto shall be paid out of the proper fund on demands duly audited, in the mode prescribed by this Charter for auditing other demands upon the Treasury. The Supervisors must also, monthly, appropriate and pay to the Trustees of the San Francisco Law Library such moneys as shall from time to time be collected by the County Clerk and paid into the Treasury for the benefit of said Law Library.

ARTICLE VIII.

Police Department.

CHAPTER I.

OF THE POLICE COMMISSIONERS.

SECTION 1. The Police Department shall be under the management of a Board of Police Commissioners, consisting of four Commissioners who shall be appointed by the Mayor and shall hold office for four years.

In making such appointments the Mayor shall not appoint more than two from the same political party. In filling any vacancy that may occur, the Mayor shall not make any appointment the result of which would cause more than two of said Commissioners to be of the same political party, and said Board shall be always so composed that there shall never be at any one time more than two Commissioners from the same political party. Those first appointed shall, immediately after their appointment, so classify themselves by lot, that they shall, respectively, go out of office at the expiration of one, two, three and four years after their appointment.

SEC. 2. Every Police Commissioner shall, after he enters on the duties of his office, continuously reside in said city and county; and any Commissioner who shall absent himself therefrom for the continuous period of sixty days, shall cease to be a Police Commissioner.

Sec. 3. No Police Commissioner shall be eligible to any other public office during his incumbency of office or for one year thereafter. No Commissioner shall, during his term of office, be a member of, or take part in, any political convention the purpose of which is to nominate candidates for office, or act as judge, inspector, clerk, or officer of any election or primary election, or take part in any election except to deposit his vote; nor shall any member of said Board, directly or indirectly, influence or attempt to influence or control the action of any member or employee of said Department in any primary, special or general election; nor shall any member of said Board receive or collect, or suffer to be received or collected, from any member of the said Department, any assessment or contribution for political purposes. A violation of any of the provisions of this section shall be cause for the immediate removal from office of the person guilty of such violation.

Sec. 4. The Police Commissioners shall meet in said city and county within ten days after their appointment and organize as a Board of Police Commissioners, and elect one of their number President, who shall hold his office for one year. The Clerk of the Chief of Police shall act as the Clerk of said Board. The sessions of said Board shall be public, except that executive sessions may be held in special cases by unanimous vote. Said Board shall meet at least once a week, in the office of the Chief of Police, or in such other place as the Supervisors shall designate, or in case of emergency, at such place as said Board may select. Every member of said Board, the Chief of Police, and the Clerk of said Board, shall have power to administer oaths in all matters pertinent to the business of their respective offices, or pending before said Board. The Board shall keep a record of its proceedings. The President, or one of the other Commissioners, shall daily visit the office of the Board.

CHAPTER II.

OF THE POWERS OF THE BOARD.

Section 1. The Police Force shall be appointed by said Board, and said Board shall have power:

1. To suspend or remove any member of said Force in the manner hereinafter provided.

2. To prescribe rules and regulations for the organization, government and discipline of said Police Force, and from time to time alter or repeal the same, and prescribe penalties for the violation of any of them.

3. To hear and summarily determine all complaints of misconduct, or inefficiency, or other charge against any member of the police force, and to take such action thereon as shall be conducive to the maintenance of the discipline and efficiency of the same.

4. To grant permits to all persons desiring to engage in the retail liquor business, upon the recommendation of the owners of a majority of the frontage of the property situated upon the same street with the proposed place of such business, and between the next adjacent cross streets, and to revoke any such permit when it shall appear to said Board that the business of the person to whom such permit was given is conducted in a disorderly or improper manner; if said Board refuse to grant such permit, or propose to revoke any permit that has been granted, the person who is refused such permit, or whose permit it proposes to revoke, shall be entitled to be heard before said Board, in person or through counsel, and to have, free of charge, all reasonable facilities for the hearing on his right to have or retain such permit. It shall not be lawful for any person to carry on the retail liquor business in said city and county without the permit hereby authorized. Such permits must be granted for not more than one year and they shall distinctly state the name of the person to whom the same is given, and a description of the premises where such business is to be carried on, and the same must be posted in a conspicuous place upon said premises. Complaints to revoke permits granted by said Board must be in writing, signed by the person making the same, and filed with the Clerk of said Board; and a copy thereof, certified by the Clerk, must be served on the party complained against at least ten days before the time for expiration of such permit, and the person holding such permit shall, before said expiration, have a hearing in opposition to such complaint.

5. At its discretion, upon the petition of any person, firm or corporation, to appoint, and at pleasure to re-

move, a special officer to do special service, to be paid for by such person, firm or corporation, specifying the boundary or locality at or within which he is to act as such special officer, which boundary or locality, together with the names of the persons, firms and corporations petitioning for such appointment, shall be described in his warrant of appointment. All special officers shall report to the Chief of Police when required by him, and be subject to his orders in case of emergency, and in no event shall such officers be paid by the city and county, or any other persons than those who shall have signed said petition, and no such special officer shall become, or obtain, bail for any person charged with any offense whatever, or recommend to any person charged with crime the employment of any particular attorney; and any such special officer who shall solicit, collect, or receive, or cause or permit others so to do for his benefit, any money or other thing, for guarding or protecting, or on pretense of so doing, the person or property of any person other than of those petitioning for his appointment as such special officer, or shall violate any of the foregoing provisions, shall be dismissed from the service.

6. To prescribe the badge of office and uniform to be worn by all members of the police force, and the badge of office to be worn by all special officers.

7. To allow and order paid out of the Police Fund, as contingent expenses of the Police Department, upon orders signed by the Chief of Police, such amount as shall be allowed by the Supervisors for that purpose; but the aggregate of such orders shall not exceed the sum of ten thousand dollars a year.

8. To appoint substitute police officers, not to exceed numerically five per centum of the police force, to serve under such regulations, and subject to such restrictions, as may be prescribed by said Board, and without pay from said city and county.

9. To issue subpœnas, tested in the name of its President, for the attendance of witnesses and production of papers upon any proceeding authorized by the rules and regulations of said Board, or by any of the provisions of this Charter, or law of the State.

10. To determine within what districts the police force shall be distributed and employed; to establish

and maintain, and at its discretion abolish stations and station houses, sub-stations and sub-station houses, for the accommodation of members of the police force, and as places of temporary detention for persons arrested.

11. Upon any emergency calling therefor, to appoint as many special patrolmen, without pay, from among citizens, as it may deem desirable. During the service of any such special patrolman, he shall possess all the powers and privileges, and perform all the duties prescribed by said Board; and every such patrolman shall wear a badge, to be prescribed and furnished by the Board.

12. To issue to every member of the police force a warrant of appointment, signed by the President and countersigned by the Clerk, which warrant shall contain the date of his appointment and his rank.

13. To report annually, on or before the first day of May, to the Supervisors an estimate of the amount of money that will be required to pay all salaries, expenses and contingent expenses of the Police Department for the ensuing fiscal year, specifying in detail the items for which the same will be required, except for those known as contingent expenses.

14. To provide for the care, restitution, or sale at public auction, of all property that may come into possession of the Property Clerk; to direct the destruction of such of said property as shall consist of lottery tickets, obscene literature, or implements, weapons and property used in the commission of crime.

15. To provide for the care, management, investment and disposition of the Police Relief and Pension Fund, and to order paid out of the same the sums hereinafter provided.

16. From the regular police force to provide for a mounted police, and make all rules and regulations necessary for the government thereof.

17. To provide for a system of patrol wagons, and also a signal system, and for such other new and useful systems as will increase the efficiency of said force.

18. To make all proper rules and regulations for carrying into execution the foregoing powers, and all other powers vested in said Department by this Charter, or by any ordinance passed pursuant thereto, or by the Constitution or laws of the State.

Sec. 2. The President shall have power to convene said Board at such time and upon such reasonable notice as he may deem fit; and the concurrence of three members shall be necessary to any decision or order of the Board. The Clerk shall have the custody of all the records and official documents of the Board.

Chapter III.

OF THE POLICE FORCE.

Section 1. The Police Force of said city and county shall consist of:

First—The Chief of Police, who shall hold office for four years, subject to removal by the said Board, and an Assistant Chief of Police appointed at the pleasure of the said Board, who shall also be Chief Inspector, and who, in case of the illness, absence or other temporary disability of the Chief of Police, shall have the same powers and perform the duties of said Chief.

Second—Six Captains of Police, one of whom may be the Assistant Chief of Police.

Third—As many Policemen, not exceeding six hundred, as the Board of Police Commissioners may with the approval of the Supervisors expressed by ordinance determine to be necessary. The members of the Police Force in service at the time this Charter goes into effect shall constitute such Police Force. Said force shall not exceed six hundred until the National Census of 1900 has been taken, after which time, should the population of said city and county exceed three hundred and fifty thousand, and the public interests require, said Board shall have power, with the approval of the Supervisors, expressed by ordinance passed by the affirmative vote of not less than nine members, to increase said Force above the number of six hundred, at the rate of one policeman for every seven hundred of population above said three hundred and fifty thousand; and said Board may at any time with the approval of the Supervisors, expressed by ordinance, decrease said Force below six hundred. When any increase of said Force is authorized as above, said Board shall have the power of appointment as in other cases. In the event of any such increase or decrease of said Force, the number of Captains, Sergeants, Corporals and Inspectors may be increased or decreased in the same proportion.

SEC. 2. In making appointments to said Force the Board shall not regard the political or partisan preference or affiliations of the candidates.

SEC. 3. Every appointee to said Force must be a citizen of the United States, of good character for honesty and sobriety, able to read and write the English language, and a resident of said city and county at least five years next preceding his appointment; every appointee to said Force hereafter appointed shall not be less than twenty-five or more than thirty-five years of age, and must possess the physical qualifications required for recruits for the United States Army, and, before his appointment, pass a satisfactory medical examination, under such rules and regulations as may be prescribed by said Board.

SEC. 4. The Chief of Police shall, from members of the Police Force, and for purposes of detective and special duty, appoint Inspectors of Police.

Any private detective or person who shall advertise or pretend to be an Inspector of Police without such appointment or authority, shall be guilty of a misdemeanor and punished therefor accordingly.

CHAPTER IV.

OF THE CHIEF OF POLICE.

SECTION 1. In the suppression of any riot, public tumult, disturbance of the public peace, or organized resistance against the laws or public authority, in the lawful exercise of his functions, the Chief of Police shall, for the time being, have all the powers that are now or may be conferred on Sheriffs by the laws of this State, and his lawful orders shall be promptly executed by all police officers and special patrolmen, if any there be, and every citizen shall when required lend him aid in the arrest and detention in custody of offenders, and the maintenance of public order. He shall keep a public office, at which, in case of his absence, a Captain of police, or police officer, by him designated for that purpose, shall be in attendance at all hours, day and night. In case of his absence from his office, it shall be made known to the police officer in attendance where he can be found. He shall designate one or more police officers to attend constantly on the Police Court, and to

execute its orders and process. He shall detail and remove at his pleasure policemen to act as his Clerk, and
as Prison Keepers and as Property Clerk. He shall supervise and direct the Police Force, and shall observe
and cause to be observed the provisions of this Charter,
and enforce within said city and county all laws of the
State applicable thereto, and all ordinances and all rules
and regulations prescribed by the said Board. He shall
see that the orders and process issued by the Police
Court are promptly executed, and shall exercise such
other powers connected with his office as may be prescribed in the general rules and regulations of the
Board. He shall acquaint himself with all statutes and
laws in force in this State defining public offenses and
nuisances, and regulating criminal proceedings, and
shall keep in his office the statutes of this State, and of
the United States, and all necessary works on criminal.
law. He shall give information and advice touching
said laws gratuitously to all police officers and magis-
trates officially asking for it.

SEC. 2. In case of great public emergency or danger,
he may, with the consent of said Board and the Supervisors, appoint during such emergency or danger and
for a limited time only, an additional number of persons of approved character for honesty and sobriety, as
policemen, who shall have the same powers for the time
being as other policemen.

SEC. 3. He may from time to time disburse such
sums for contingent expenses of said Department as in
his judgment shall be for the best interest of the city
and county, to be paid out of the contingent expenses
allowed said Department; but the aggregate of all such
sums shall not in any one fiscal year exceed the sum of
ten thousand dollars, and all sums so disbursed shall be
subject to the approval of said Board.

SEC. 4. He shall have full control and direction of
all members of the Police Force in the lawful exercise
of his functions, with full power to detail any of them
to such public service as he may direct, and with like
power to temporarily suspend any member or officer on
said Force, but in all cases of such suspension he shall
promptly report the same to the Board, with the reason
therefor in writing.

SEC. 5. Every member of said Force shall provide-himself with the uniform prescribed by the regulations of the Board, which shall be worn on all occasions while on duty, with such exceptions as may be permitted by the Chief of Police in the performance of detective duty. The Chief of Police shall maintain and enforce rigid discipline, so as to secure the complete efficiency of said Force.

Chapter V.

OF THE DUTIES OF POLICEMEN.

Section 1. Policemen, in subjection to the orders of their respective Captains, under the general direction of the Chief of Police, must be prompt and vigilant in the detection of crime, the arrest of public offenders, the suppression of all riots, frays, duels and disturbance of the public peace, the execution of process from the Police Court, in causing the abatement of public nuisances, and the enforcement of the laws and the ordinances of said city and county, and shall report in writing to the Chief of Police, daily, any infraction thereof.

Sec. 2. Each member of the Police Force, under the penalty of a fine of fifteen days' pay, or dismissal from the Force, at the discretion of the Board, shall, immediately upon making an arrest, convey in person the offender before the nearest sitting magistrate, that he may be dealt with according to law. If the arrest is made at a time when the magistrate is not holding Court, such offender may be detained in a station house until the next public sitting of the magistrate, and no longer, and shall then be conveyed without delay before a magistrate, to be dealt with according to law; and said Board shall make rules and regulations to prevent the undue detention of persons arrested.

Sec. 3. Every member of the Police Force shall take and subscribe the constitutional oath of office before entering upon the duties of his office.

Sec. 4. Every policeman shall, on the arrest of any notorious or dangerous offender, or any person charged with the commission of a grave crime, search the person of such offender, and take from him all property and weapons, and forthwith deliver the same to the Prison Keeper, who must deliver the same to the Property Clerk, to be by him kept until other disposition be made thereof according to law. All persons arrested for drunkenness, and who are in an apparently stupefied or senseless condition, must be examined by the City Physician or the Assistant City Physician before being placed in a cell, and if upon such examination such person shall not be found intoxicated, or if otherwise necessary, he or she shall be conveyed to one of the receiving hospitals and placed under medical treatment.

SEC. 5. No member of the Police Department shall be eligible to any other office while connected with such Force, nor shall he take any part whatever in any convention held for the purposes of a political party; nor shall he be a member of any political club. No member of said Force shall interfere with politics on an election day, or at any other time while employed on said Force. No member of said Force, while on duty, shall enter any liquor saloon, bar-room or place where liquors are retailed, except in the discharge of his duties. Any violation of any of the provisions of this section shall be cause for removal from office.

SEC. 6. No member of the Police Force shall engage in any other profession or calling, become bail for any person charged with any offense whatever, recommend to persons charged with crime the employment of any particular attorney, receive any present or reward for services rendered, or to be rendered, unless with the approbation of a majority of the Board, expressed in writing; or be allowed pay for any period during which he has been absent from duty, unless such absence resulted from sickness, or from disability occasioned by injuries received in the discharge of his official duty.

SEC. 7. Any member of said Force, soliciting, collecting or receiving, or causing or permitting others to do so for his benefit, any money or other thing, for guarding or protecting, or on pretence of so doing, the person or property of any person, shall be dismissed from the service, except that special police officers shall be subject, as to compensation and reward, to the provisions of Subdivision 5, of Section 1, of Chapter II, of this Article.

Chapter VI.

OF SUSPENSIONS AND REMOVALS.

Section 1. Any member of the Police Force guilty of any legal offense, neglect of duty, violation of rules, or neglect or disobedience of orders, or inefficiency, or absence without leave, or conduct injurious to the public peace or welfare, or immoral conduct, or conduct unbecoming an officer, or breach of discipline, shall be liable to be punished by reprimand, forfeiting pay for a specified time, or dismissal from the Force; but no more than fifteen days' pay shall be forfeited for any one offense. All moneys so forfeited shall be for the benefit of the Police Relief and Pension Fund.

Sec. 2. Members of said Force shall be subject to removal or punishment for any of the reasons specified in the preceding section, only upon trial before the Board of Police Commissioners. Charges when presented by the Chief of Police, or a Captain, or a Sergeant of Police, or in a verified complaint by any person, setting forth the specific acts complained of, shall be received, considered and determined by said Board, giving to the accused such reasonable notice as it may prescribe, and an impartial hearing in his defense; and upon such hearing the accused shall have the right to be heard in person or by counsel. Upon such trial, said Board shall furnish the accused with all reasonable facilities for the conduct of his defense, and secure to him, free of charge, the attendance of all witnesses reasonably necessary for his defense.

Chapter VII.

OF LOST OR STOLEN PROPERTY.

Section 1. All property or money alleged or supposed to have been feloniously obtained, or which has been lost or abandoned, and which shall hereafter be taken into the custody of any member of the Police Force, or of any Criminal Court in said City and County or any Police Judge, shall be by such member, Court or Judge, given into the custody of the Property Clerk. All such property and money shall be registered by such Clerk in a book kept for that purpose, which shall also contain a record of the names of the persons from whom such property or money was taken, the names of all claimants thereto, the time of the seizure, and the disposition thereof.

SEC. 2. When property or money shall be taken from any person arrested, and it be alleged that it was feloniously obtained, or is the proceeds of crime, and it is brought with the claimant thereof, and the person arrested before a Judge or Court for adjudication, and the Judge or Court shall be satisfied that the person arrested is innocent of the offense alleged, and that the property belongs to him, said Court or Judge may thereupon, in writing, order such property or money to be returned, and the Property Clerk to deliver such property or money to the accused, personally, but not to any attorney, agent or clerk of such person.

SEC. 3. If any claim to the ownership of such property or money shall be made on oath before such Judge or Court, by or on behalf of any person other than the person arrested, and the accused person shall be held for trial or examination, such property or money shall remain in the custody of the Property Clerk until the discharge or conviction of the person accused.

SEC. 4. All property or money taken on suspicion of having been feloniously obtained, or being the proceeds of crime, and for which there is no other claimant than the person from whom such property was taken, and all lost property coming into the possession of any member of said Force, and all property and money taken from pawnbrokers as the proceeds of crime, or taken from persons supposed to be insane, intoxicated or otherwise incapable of taking care of themselves, shall be delivered as soon as practicable to the Property Clerk.

SEC. 5. All unclaimed property and money that has been in the custody of the Property Clerk for the period of one year, shall be sold at public auction, after having been three times advertised in the official newspaper; and the proceeds of such sale shall be paid into the Treasury to the credit of the Police Relief and Pension Fund. When it is necessary to use such property as evidence it shall not be sold or disposed of until the necessity for the use thereof as evidence has ceased, and thereupon it shall be disposed of as hereinbefore provided. The proceeds of property taken from persons supposed to be insane, shall not become part of said

10

Fund until after the expiration of three years from the time when the same shall come into the Treasury. The Chief of Police and said Board, immediately after the seizure or finding of any property of any such supposed insane person, must endeavor to find the guardian or other person entitled to the possession of such property, or the proceeds thereof, and deliver the same to him; but if such person cannot be found, and the proceeds of said property remain unclaimed for said period of three years, then the same shall become part of said Fund.

SEC. 6. If any property or money in the custody of the Property Clerk be required as evidence in any Court, it shall be delivered to any officer who shall present an order, in writing, to that effect, from such Court. Such property or money, shall not be retained in such Court, but be returned to said Property Clerk.

SEC. 7. All property and money in the custody of the Property Clerk shall be deposited by him for safe keeping with the Treasurer of the said city and county in such manner and subject to such rules and regulations as may be prescribed by the said Board.

CHAPTER VIII.

OF THE POLICE RELIEF AND PENSON FUND.

SECTION 1. The Board of Police Commissioners of the City and County of San Francisco, and their successors in office, shall constitute a Board of Trustees of the Fund herein provided for and known as the Police Relief or Pension Fund of the Police Department; they shall provide for the disbursement of the same and designate the beneficiaries thereof, as hereinafter directed, which Board shall be known as the " Board of Police Pension Fund Commissioners."

SEC. 2. They shall organize as such Board by choosing one of their number as Chairman, and by appointing a Secretary. The Treasurer of the City and County shall be *ex officio* Treasurer of said fund. Such Board of Trustees shall have charge of and administer said fund, and order payments therefrom in pursuance of the provisions of this Act. They shall report annually in the month of June, to the Board of Supervisors of said City and County, the condition of the said Police Relief and Pension Fund, and the receipts and disbursements on account of the same, with a full and complete list of the beneficiaries of said fund and the amounts paid them.

SEC. 3. Whenever any person at the taking effect of this Charter or thereafter shall have been duly appointed and sworn, and have served for the period of twenty years or more as a member in any capacity or any rank whatever of the regularly constituted police department of said city and county, said Board shall be empowered to order and direct that such person shall, after becom-becoming sixty years of age and his service in such Police Department shall have ceased, be paid from such fund a yearly pension equal to one-half the amount of salary attached to the rank which he may have held in said Police Department for one year next preceding the expiration of said term of twenty years, but such pension shall at once cease and determine upon the death of the person receiving the same.

SEC. 4. Whenever any person while serving as policeman in said city and county, shall become physically disabled by reason of bodily injury received in the performance of his duty as such policeman, said Board may upon his written request, or without such request, if it deem for the good of said Police Force, retire such person from said department, and order and direct that he shall be paid from said fund a yearly pension equal to one-half the amount of the salary attached to the rank which he may have held on such Police Force preceding such retirement, but after the death of such pensioner, his heirs or assigns are to receive no compensation whatever.

SEC. 5. No person shall be retired, as provided in the next preceding section, or receive any benefit from said fund, unless there shall be filed with said Board, certificates of such disability, which certificates shall be subscribed and sworn by said person and by the City and County Physician and two regularly licensed physicians of said city and county, and said Board may require other evidence of such dsiability before ordering such retirement and payment as aforesaid.

SEC. 6. Whenever any member of the Police Department of said city and county shall lose his life while in the performance of his duty, leaving a widow or child or children under the age of sixteen years, then upon satisfactory proofs of such facts made to it, such Board shall order and direct that a yearly pension equal to one-third the amount of the salary attached to the rank which such member held in said Police Department at the time of his death, shall be paid to such widow during her life, or if no widow, then the child or children, until they shall be sixteen years of age; *provided*, if such widow, or child or children, shall marry, then such person so marrying shall thereafter receive no further pension from such fund.

SEC. 7. Whenever any member of the Police Department of said city and county shall, after ten years' service, die from natural causes, then his widow or children, or if there be no widow or children, then his mother, if dependent upon him for support, shall be entitled to a sum equal to the amount retained by the Treasurer of said city and county from the pay of such deceased member and paid into the said Police Relief and Pension Fund.

SEC. 8. All members of the Police Force who may be retired under the provisions of this Charter shall report to the Chief of Police of said city and county on the first Mondays of April, July, October and January of each year.

SEC. 9. When any person who shall have received any benefit from said fund shall be convicted of any felony he shall forfeit all his right, claim and interest to any of the benefits allowed by this fund.

SEC. 10. The Board herein provided for shall hold quarterly meetings on the first Mondays of April, July, October and January of each year, and upon the call of its President; it shall biennially select from its members a President; it shall issue warrants signed by its President and Secretary, to the persons entitled thereto of the amount of money ordered paid to such persons from such fund by said Board, which warrant shall state for what purpose such payment is to be made; it shall keep a record of all its proceedings, which record shall be a public record; it shall at each quarterly meeting send to the Treasurer of said city and county and to the Auditor of said city and county a written or printed list of all persons entitled to payment from the fund herein provided for, stating the amount of such payments and for what granted, which list shall be certified and signed by the President and Secretary of such Board, attested under oath. The Auditor shall thereupon enter a copy of said list upon a book to be kept for that purpose, and which shall be known as "The Police Relief and Pension Fund" book. When such list has been entered by the Auditor he shall transmit the same to the Board of Supervisors, which Board shall order the payment of the amounts named therein out of "The Police Relief and Pension Fund." A majority of all the members of said Board herein provided for shall constitute a quorum and have power to transact business.

Sec. 11. The Board herein provided for shall, in addition to other powers herein granted, have power:

First—To compel witnesses to attend and testify before it, upon all matters connected with the operation of this Charter, in the same manner as is or may be provided by law for the taking of testimony before Notaries Public; and its President, or any member of said Board, may administer oaths to such witnesses.

Second—To appoint a Secretary, and to provide for the payment from said fund of all its necessary expenses, not exceeding fifty dollars for any one month, including the salary of the Secretary, and printing; provided that no compensation or emolument shall be paid to any member of said Board for any duty required or performed under this Charter.

Third—To make all needful rules and regulations for its guidance, in conformity with the provisions of this Charter.

Sec. 12. The Board of Supervisors of said City and County, for the purpose of said "Police Relief and Pension Fund" hereinbefore mentioned, shall annually, when the tax levy is made, direct the payment into said fund, of the following moneys:

First—Not less than five nor more than ten per centum of all moneys collected and received from licenses for the keeping of places wherein spirituous, malt, or other intoxicating liquors are sold.

Second—One-half of all moneys received from taxes or from licenses upon dogs.

Third—All moneys received from fines imposed upon members of the police force of said city and county for violation of the rules and regulations of the Police Department.

Fourth—All proceeds of sales of unclaimed property.

Fifth—Not less than one-fourth nor more than one-half of all moneys received from licenses from pawnbrokers, billiard-hall keepers, second-hand dealers, and junk stores.

Sixth—All moneys received from fines for carrying concealed weapons.

Seventh—Twenty-five per centum of all fines collected in money for violation of said city and county ordinances.

Eighth—All rewards given or paid to members of such police force, except such as shall be excepted by the Chief of Police.

Ninth—The Treasurer of said city and county shall retain from the pay of each member of the Police Department, the sum of two dollars per month, to be forthwith paid into said "Police Relief and Pension Fund," and no other or further retention or deduction shall be made from such pay for any other fund or purpose whatever.

Sec. 13. On the last day of June of each year, or as soon thereafter as practicable, the Auditor of said city and county shall make a report to the Board of Supervisors, of said city and county, of all moneys paid out on account of said fund during the previous year and of the amount then to the credit of the "Police Relief and Pension Fund" and all surplus of said fund then remaining in said fund exceeding the average amount per year paid out on account of said fund during the three years next preceding, shall be transferred to and become a part of the surplus fund of said city and county, and no longer under the control of said Board, or subject to its order. Payments provided for in this Act shall be made quarterly upon proper vouchers.

Sec. 14. Nothing in this chapter shall be so construed as to give to any member, or retired member, of the Board of Police Commissioners the right to participate or share in any of the benefits of the said Police Relief and Pension Fund, either as members of the police force or in any capacity, or on any ground whatsoever. The provisions of this section shall not apply to the Chief of Police in the event of his having been, *ex officio* or otherwise, a member of the said Board under any previous law.

CHAPTER IX.

OF THE FIRE MARSHAL.

SECTION 1. The Board of Police Commissioners, upon the written recommendation of the Board of Directors of the corporation known as the "Underwriters' Fire Patrol of San Francisco," may appoint such persons as may be recommended by said Board of Directors, as Fire Marshal and Assistant Fire Marshal, to be known as public officers. Any vacancy occurring in the office of Fire Marshal or Assistant Fire Marshal shall be filled in the same manner. Said Board of Police Commissioners may revoke any such appointments at any time.

SEC. 2. Said Fire Marshal shall attend all fires which may occur in said city and county, with his badge of office conspicuously displayed, and shall as far as practicable, protect all property which may be imperiled at any such fire, and prevent such property from being injured.

SEC. 3. Said Fire Marshal may appoint one or more persons during the time of fire for the purpose of saving and protecting property thereat, and until it shall be delivered to the owner or claimant thereof; said owner or claimant shall pay all actual expenses incurred by said Fire Marshal for the preservation and keeping of the same; but no expense of caring for and protecting such property for more than twenty-four hours shall be charged to the owner or claimant provided they can be found within the said time, when such property is not insured. If such property be insured no charge shall be made therefor. Said person or persons, so appointed, shall have, during such period, the authority and power of a policeman; and shall be known as the Fire Marshal's Police; and each of such persons shall wear, while in the discharge of duty, conspicuously displayed on his person, such badge as the Board of Police Commissioners may designate.

SEC. 4. Said Fire Marshal shall investigate the cause of all such fires, and in all cases where he shall believe that a crime has been committed, make a written report of such investigation to the District Attorney.

SEC. 5. Said Fire Marshal shall exercise the functions of a police officer, and in all investigations of the causes of such fires as shall occur he shall have power to issue

subpœnas and administer oaths, and compel the attendance of witnesses before him. All subpœnas issued by
said Fire Marshal shall be in such form as he may prescribe. Such subpœnas shall be served by any police
officer when thereunto authorized by the Chief of
Police. Any witness who refuses to attend or testify in
obedience to such subpœnas shall be guilty of contempt, and punishable as for contempt in Justices'
Courts. Any person who shall be guilty of false swearing
in any investigation by said Fire Marshal, shall be
deemed guilty of perjury.

SEC. 6. Said Fire Marshal is hereby duly authorized
and empowered to hold and sell, or cause to be sold, at
public auction, all property in his possession saved from
the fire, for which no owner can be found. The proceeds of all such sales, together with an account thereof,
after deducting all expenses, shall be by him deposited
with the Treasurer of said city and county, to be held
by said Treasurer subject to the claim of the owner of
such property, for a period of two years. At the expiration of that time, if not claimed, it shall be paid over
to the Firemen's Relief and Pension Fund, to be devoted to the general purposes of said fund. And said
Fire Marshal shall from time to time file with the County
Clerk of said city and county, under oath, a statement
and description of all property in his possession, or
under his control and sold by him, together with the
amount of money deposited with the Treasurer of said
city and county, as the proceeds of any sale or sales he
may have made.

SEC. 7. Said Fire Marshal shall aid in the enforcement of the fire ordinances, and for this purpose may
visit and examine all buildings in process of construction
or undergoing repair. He shall have and exercise all the
powers of a Fire Warden. Said Fire Marshal, by and
with the consent of the Board of Police Commissioners,
may appoint not exceeding six deputies, to aid him in the
discharge of his duties; said deputies to be nominated
by said Board of Directors of said Fire Patrol.

He shall exercise such other powers as may be conferred upon him by ordinance; and the Supervisors
may, from time to time, enact such ordinances as will
enable him to fully carry out the object and purposes of
this chapter.

Sec. 8. The Chief of Police may detail such police officers as he may deem necessary to enable said Fire Marshal to effectually perform his duties, and when so detailed said police officers shall aid him in the performance of his duties.

Sec. 9. Any person who willfully hinders or obstructs said Fire Marshal in the lawful discharge or performance of any of the duties of his office shall be deemed guilty of a misdemeanor, and, on conviction thereof, shall be punished by imprisonment in the County Jail for not more than three months, or by fine not exceeding $500; *provided*, however, that nothing herein contained shall be so construed as to authorize said Fire Marshal to interfere in any manner with the discharge of the lawful duties and authority of the Police or Fire Department.

Sec. 10. In the absence of said Fire Marshal from a fire, or in case of his inability to perform his duties, said Assistant Fire Marshal shall perform such duties for the time being.

Sec. 11. The salary and pay of said Fire Marshal and Assistant Fire Marshal, and of said Deputies, shall be fixed and paid by said Board of Directors of said " Underwriters' Fire Patrol of San Francisco," and in no event shall the city and county be liable therefor, or for any part thereof.

ARTICLE IX.

Fire Department.

CHAPTER 1.

ORGANIZATION AND POWERS.

Section 1. The Fire Department shall be under the management of a Board of Fire Commissioners consisting of four persons, who shall be appointed by the Mayor, and shall hold office for four years, subject to removal by him. In making such appointments the Mayor shall not appoint more than two of such Commissioners from the same political party. The Mayor shall also fill any vacancy, and such appointee shall hold office for the unexpired term that may occur, but said Board shall be always so composed that there shall never be at any one time more than two Commissioners of the same political party. Those first appointed shall so classify themselves by lot at their first meeting, which shall be within ten days after their appointment, that they shall respectively go out of office at the end of one, two, three and four years after their appointment. No Fire Commissioner shall be eligible to any office under the City and County or State Government, during the term for which he shall have been appointed to the office of Fire Commissioner, nor for one year thereafter. Immediately after the qualification of the Commissioners they shall organize by electing one of their number President, who shall hold such office for the term of one year, and they shall appoint a Secretary, which said Secretary shall also be the Secretary of the Chief Engineer and head of the clerical force of said Department and bureaus thereof, and shall perform such other duties as said Board shall prescribe.

Said Board shall meet at least once in each week, or as often as the business of the Department may require, and all their meetings shall be public. The President or one of the other Commissioners shall daily visit the office of the Board.

SEC. 2. Said Board shall supervise and possess full power and authority over all funds, moneys and appropriations, made for the use of the Fire Department, and also of the organization, government and discipline of said Department and the bureaus thereof, and shall, subject to the laws and ordinances governing said Department, prescribe the duties of the officers, members, employees, and prescribe a uniform and badge of office to be worn by them. And said Board shall have control of all the property and equipments belonging to said Department.

SEC. 3. All officers, members and employees of said Department and the bureaus thereof shall be appointed by said Board of Fire Commissioners, and shall retain their positions during good behavior, and they shall be appointed from the force of the Fire Department and Fire Alarm and Police Telegraph, as constituted at the time of the adoption and enforcement of this Charter.

SEC. 4. All persons appointed in said Department must be citizens of the United States, of good character for honesty and sobriety, able to read and write the English language, and residents of said city and county at least three years next preceding their appointment, at least twenty-one years of age, and must, before their appointment, pass a medical examination under such rules and regulations as may be prescribed by said Board of Fire Commissioners, and upon such examination must be found in sound bodily health.

SEC. 5. No officer, member or employee of said Department or bureaus thereof, shall be appointed or removed because of his political faith or opinion, nor shall he be dismissed except for cause, nor until after a trial, as hereinafter provided.

SEC. 6. Said Board of Fire Commissioners shall see that the officers, members and employees of said Department and the bureaus thereof, faithfully discharge their duties, and that the laws, ordinances and regulations are carried into effect; and they shall make all rules and regulations necessary to secure discipline and efficiency in said Department and bureaus thereof; and to enable it to enforce such rules and regulations it may impose reasonable fines and forfeitures upon the officers, members and employees for a violation thereof, or such other punishment as said Board may by rule prescribe. Said fines and forfeitures imposed as aforesaid, shall be deducted from their monthly warrant or warrants, and shall be kept by the Treasurer in the Fireman's Relief and Pension Fund.

SEC. 7. The said Fire Department shall consist of three bureaus; one bureau shall be charged with the duties of extinguishing fires, the principal officer of which shall be called the Chief Engineer of the Department. Another bureau shall be charged with the execution of all laws and ordinances relating to the storage, sale and use of combustible materials and explosives and with the execution of all laws and codes relating to the construction and alteration of buildings. The principal officer shall be called Inspector of Combustibles and Buildings. Another bureau shall be known as the Fire Alarm and Police Telegraph, the principal officer of which shall be called the Superintendent of Fire Alarm and Police Telegraph, and shall have charge of the Fire Alarm and Police Telegraph, and, in addition thereto, shall enforce all laws and orders now existing or made hereafter relating to the erection and construction of all electric wires in said city and county, public or private.

Sec. 8. No article whatever shall be delivered to said Department except upon a requisition signed by the Chief Engineer and Secretary of the Board of Fire Commissioners; and the Clerk of the Supply Department at the Fire Department Corporation Yard shall not deliver any supplies or stores pertaining to said Department to any officer, member or employee, except upon an order signed by the Chief Engineer and the Secretary of the said Board of Fire Commissioners; *provided*, that pending a conflagration such material or apparatus as may be required for the purpose of extinguishing such conflagration, may be withdrawn from the Fire Department Corporation Yard by order of the Chief Engineer, or principal officer in charge of the force of the Department at such conflagration.

Sec. 9. The Board of Supervisors of the city and county is hereby authorized and empowered to appropriate, allow and set aside annually, such sum or sums of money as the Board of Fire Commissioners determine necessary for the maintenance of the Department for the ensuing fiscal year.

Sec. 10. Every claim against said Fire Department Fund shall be approved by said Board of Fire Commissioners, and no claim of any character whatever against said fund shall be allowed or ordered paid until the same has been approved and passed by said Board of Fire Commissioners in open session, on a call of the ayes and noes, which approval shall be entered in the minutes of the Board and a certificate that the claim has been so approved shall be entered on the claim and signed by the President and Secretary of said Board before the same can be allowed by the Auditor or paid by the Treasurer.

Chapter II.

DUTIES OF THE CHIEF ENGINEER.

Section 1. The Chief Engineer of the Department shall determine and report to the Board of Fire Commissioners, as to the necessity of constructing cisterns, or erecting hydrants in particular localities, also as to the necessity for new or additional buildings, apparatus and fire boats and for materials, supplies, engines, hose, horses, houses, hook and ladders, fire extinguishers and other apparatus, and also as to the alterations and repairs to the same and as to the material required for the efficient working of the various bureaus of said Department, also as to the number of companies, officers, members and employees necessary in the various bureaus thereof. But the action of the Chief Engineer with respect to the necessity of these matters, shall only be advisory to said Board of Fire Commissioners, and no increase nor decrease in the buildings, apparatus, material, companies, officers, members or employees or other matters shall be made until the same shall have been authorized by the Board of Fire Commissioners in open meeting.

CHAPTER III.

CONTRACTS.

SECTION 1. All contracts involving an expenditure of over five hundred dollars shall be let and ordered by the Board of Fire Commissioners by bids, and said Board shall supervise all said work done, and contracts let for the Fire Department and various bureaus thereof, except work authorized by this Charter to be done under the supervision and control of other departments of the City Government; and said Board of Fire Commissioners shall see that all contracts awarded and work done for said Department are faithfully performed. The Board of Fire Commissioners shall, upon the awarding of any such contract, exact a bond that, in their judgment, is satisfactory and adequate for the prompt and faithful performance of such contract.

SEC. 2. The Board of Supervisors is authorized and required to provide and furnish for the use of said Board of Fire Commissioners, Fire Department and the various bureaus thereof, suitable rooms in some of the public buildings, for the transaction of the business of the said Department and the various bureaus thereof.

CHAPTER IV.

DUTIES OF THE COMMISSIONERS.

SECTION 1. The clerical force of said Department shall be in attendance at their headquarters daily, which shall be from nine A. M. until five P. M. during office hours.

The Chief Engineer and such officers as the Board of Fire Commissioners may prescribe, shall be at the headquarters of said Department, daily during office hours, when not otherwise engaged in their official duties.

SEC. 2. The Board of Fire Commissioners shall furnish such horses and vehicles to the Chief Engineer and other officers and employees of said Department or of the various bureaus thereof, as may be required in the performance of their official duties, and provide for the keeping of the same.

SEC. 3. The Board of Fire Commissioners is also authorized to establish and maintain at the Corporation Yard of said Department, a workshop, for making, repairing and improving the apparatus of said Department, and may allow and order paid out of the amount allowed to be expended for said purpose the necessary expense of said workshop and the salaries of the employees thereof.

SEC. 4. The Fire Department and the various bureaus thereof, shall consist of such officers, members and employees, and such engine, hose, hook and ladder, chemical engine, and water tower companies as may be organized and in operation in said Fire Department, and Fire Alarm and Police Telegraph, at the time of the adoption and enforcement of this Charter.

SEC. 5. The Board of Fire Commissioners shall divide said city and county into districts, and assign one of the battalion chiefs to each district, and he shall reside in the district to which he has been assigned, and shall be responsible for the condition of the apparatus and discipline of the officers and members therein.

SEC. 6. The Chief Engineer shall be the executive officer of said department and of the various bureaus thereof, and it shall be his duty and that of the Assistant Chief Engineers, and of the battalion chiefs, to see that all laws, orders, rules and regulations, in force in said city and county, or made by the Board of Fire Commissioners, concerning said department or the various bureaus thereof, are enforced.

SEC. 7. The Chief Engineer may suspend any subordinate officer, member or employee of said department or the various bureaus thereof, for incompetency or for any violations of the rules and regulations of said Department and shall forthwith report in writing, with his reasons therefore, to the Board of Fire Commissioners for its action. He shall diligently observe the condition of the apparatus and workings of the Department, and report in writing thereon, at least once in each month, to said Board, and make such recommendations and suggestions respecting the same as he may deem proper; and in the absence, or inability to act, of the Chief Engineer, the First Assistant Chief Engineer shall perform the duties of the office of the Chief Engineer, and in the absence or inability of both said officers, the Second Assistant Chief Engineer shall perform the duties of said office.

SEC. 8. The Chief Engineer, or in his absence, the Assistant Chief Engineers, or in their absence any battalion chief in charge, may, during a conflagration, cause to be cut down, or otherwise removed, any building or structure for the purpose of checking the progress of such conflagration.

SEC. 9. In all investigations and trials for violation of the rules and regulations of said department or the various bureaus thereof, the President of the Board of Fire Commissioners shall have power to issue subpœnas, administer oaths and affirmations and compel the attendance of witnesses before said Board, by attachment or otherwise; all subpœnas issued by him shall be in such form as he may prescribe, and shall be served by any police officer or any peace officer of said city and county. Any witness who shall neglect or refuse to attend or testify in obedience to such subpœna, shall be deemed guilty of contempt, and shall be punishable by him, as in cases of contempt in justices courts in civil cases. In the absence of the President, any member of said Board may act in his place and stead, and shall have full power and authority to perform all the duties pertaining to said office.

No officer, member or employee of said Department shall be dismissed, except for cause, nor until after a trial. The accused shall be furnished with a written copy of the charges against him, at least three days previous to the day of trial; and he shall have an opportunity to examine witnesses in his behalf, and all witnesses shall be examined under oath, and all trials shall be public.

SEC. 10. All officers of the Fire Department while

on duty shall be vested with all the powers of arrest and detention and other constabulary authority vested in police officers.

SEC. 11. The Board of Fire Commissioners shall not, nor shall either of them, nor shall any officer, member or employee of said Fire Department and the various bureaus thereof, receive any gratuity or advantage from any contractor, laborer or person performing labor for, or furnishing materials or supplies to said Department. Any violation of the provisions of this section shall be sufficient cause for the removal of the Commissioner, officer, member or employee, guilty of such violation. And all contracts made and entered into, in violation of the same, shall be void.

SEC. 12. No member of said Board of Fire Commissioners shall, during his term of office, be a member of any convention held for political purposes, nor shall any officer, member or employee of said Department take any part whatever in any convention held for political purposes, or be a member of any political club, association or organization, or take any part whatever in any primary or general election, other than to exercise his individual suffrage at such general election. Nor shall they or either of them levy, collect or pay any money, as an assessment or as a voluntary contribution, for political purposes.

Any Commissioner, officer, member or employee of the Department, violating any of the provisions of this section, shall forfeit his position or office.

SEC. 13. Whenever an officer, member or employee of said Department shall become disabled, by reason of injuries received at a fire, so as to be unable to perform his duties, said Board of Fire Commissioners may allow said disabled person a sum not exceeding fifty dollars per month, for a time not exceeding three months.

SEC. 14. At the beginning of the fiscal year next succeeding the adoption and enforcement of this Charter, the Board of Fire Commissioners shall reorganize the Fire Department and Fire Alarm and Police Telegraph of this city and county so as to conform to the provisions of this Charter, and in so doing said Board shall appoint as such officers, members and employees those persons now constituting the officers, members and employees of the same; *provided*, that where in this article any reduction is made in the force, or in the companies thereof, or in the office of the Fire Alarm and Police Telegraph, the said Board of Fire Commissioners is authorized to discharge from the said Department and Fire Alarm and Police Telegraph those persons whose discharge in their judgment shall be most conducive to the efficient reorganization of said Fire Department and Fire Alarm and Police Telegraph; and until such reorganization is made in said Fire Department and Fire Alarm and Police Telegraph said Departments shall remain organized according to the laws in force at the time this Charter takes effect.

CHAPTER V.

OFFICERS AND EMPLOYEES.

SECTION 1. The officers of the Fire Department, until otherwise provided, shall be:

One Chief Engineer.

Two Assistant Chief Engineers.

One Chief for each Battalion.

One Secretary and Chief Clerk.

One Assistant Secretary and Clerk.

One Clerk.

One Clerk of Supply Department.

One Chief of Bureau of Combustibles, Explosives and Buildings.

One Superintendent of Fire Alarm and Police Telegraph.

One Superintendent of Engines.

One Assistant Superintendent of Engines.

One Captain for each Company.

One Lieutenant for each Company.

Which said officers may be increased or diminished by the Board of Fire Commissioners as the demands of the Department or the growth of the city may require.

The members of said Department shall be:

One Foreman Machinist.

Three Hydrantmen.

Two Draymen.

Two Hostlers.

One Watchman.

One Veterinary Surgeon.

One Foreman Carpenter.

11

Two Telegraph Operators for Chief and First Assistant.

And all Drivers, Stokers, Tillermen, Stewards, Firemen, Pilots, Hosemen and Truckmen as hereinafter provided.

The officers, members and employees of the Fire Alarm and Police Telegraph shall be:

One Superintendent, as hereinbefore provided.

One Chief Operator.

Three Operators.

Two Assistant Operators.

One Foreman of Construction and Repairs.

One Assistant Foreman.

One Repairer.

Three Inspectors.

Four Linemen.

Two Batterymen.

And such other assistance as the Chief Engineer may deem necessary, but such recommendation must have the approval of the Board of Fire Commissioners.

SEC. 2. The Board of Fire Commissioners is authorized to provide, erect and maintain a training school for firemen, on some suitable lot belonging to said city and county, and shall prescribe rules and regulations for the management of the same.

SEC. 3. The Board of Fire Commissioners may pension and retire from active service any aged, infirm or disabled fireman, in accordance with the provisions of an Act entitled, "An Act to authorize the Board of Supervisors or other governing authority of the different counties, cities and counties, cities and towns of the State, to provide pensions or benefits for the relief of aged, infirm or disabled firemen." Approved March 11, 1889.

SEC. 4. Each Steam Fire Engine Company shall be composed of not more than One Captain, One Lieutenant, One Engineer, One Driver, One Stoker and Five Hosemen.

Each Hook and Ladder Company shall be composed of not more than One Captain, One Lieutenant, One Driver, One Tillerman and Eight Truckmen.

Each Hose Company shall be composed of not more than One Captain, One Lieutenant, One Driver, One Steward and Five Hosemen.

Each Chemical Engine Company shall be composed of not more than One Captain, One Lieutenant, One Driver and One Hoseman.

Each Water Tower Company shall be composed of not more than One Captain, One Driver and One Hosemen.

Each Fire Boat Company shall be composed of not more than One Captain, One Lieutenant, One Engineer, One Assistant Engineer, Two Firemen, One Pilot and Twelve Hosemen.

CHAPTER VI.

OF THE FIREMEN'S RELIEF AND PENSION FUND.

SECTION 1. The Firemen's Relief and Pension Fund shall consist of the moneys paid into said Fund, as in the next section provided; of fines collected from members of said Department and of such other moneys as may be contributed thereto by gift, devise, bequest or otherwise. Said Fund shall be under the control and management of the Board of Fire Commissioners.

SEC. 2. On the first Monday in each month there shall be transferred by the Treasurer from the General Fund to the Firemen's Relief and Pension Fund a sum aggregating two dollars for each officer and member regularly enrolled in the Fire Department. A certificate, under oath, of such enrollment must be furnished monthly by the Secretary of the Board of Fire Commissioners to the Auditor and Treasurer.

SEC. 3. Said Board may, from time to time, invest the moneys of said Fund in such of the following securities as shall seem most safe and profitable; the bonds of the City and County of San Francisco; the bonds of the State of California; the bonds of the United States of America, or the bonds of any city or county in the State of California; *provided*, that the validity and safety of such securities have been properly examined and approved by the City Treasurer, or it may loan at interest the whole or any portion of said moneys upon said securities. The securities and evidences of any such loan shall be delivered to and held by the Treasurer, who shall be responsible therefor on his official bond, and he shall not deposit, pledge or in any way part with any of said securities or the evidences of any such loan except on the order of said Board. Upon making any such investment or loan, said Board shall immediately make a report thereof in writing, with all particulars, to the Auditor.

SEC. 4. Said Board may, by a unanimous vote relieve from service at fires or retire from all service in the Fire Department, any officer or member thereof who shall, upon an examination by a physician designated by said Board, be found to be disqualified, physically or mentally, for the performance of his duties; and said officer or member so retired from service, shall receive from said Fund as hereinafter provided, an annual allowance as pension in case of total disqualification for service or as compensation for limited service in case of partial disability. Said pension or allowance shall be in lieu of such salary as he may have previously received. The amount of such pension or allowance shall be determined as follows: In case of total permanent disability, caused in or induced by the actual performance of his duties, or which may occur after ten years' actual and continuous service in said Department, the amount of annual pension to be allowed shall not be more than one-third of the annual salary received by such officer or member at the date of his retirement from service, or such less sum in proportion to the number of persons in receipt of an allowance from said Fund as its conditions shall warrant, the same to be determined, and increased or diminished from time to time by said Board. In case of partial permanent disability caused in or induced by the actual performance of the duties of his position, or which may occur after five years' active and continuous service in said Department, the officer or member so disabled may be relieved from active service at fires, but shall remain an employee of the Department, subject to the rules governing the same, and to the performance of such duties as the physician designated by the said Board may certify that he is qualified to perform; and the annual compensation to be paid to such officer or member shall not be more than one-third in amount of the annual salary received by him at the date of his being relieved from active service, or such less sum in proportion to the number of persons receiving an allowance from said Fund as its condition will warrant, the same to be determined, and increased or diminished from time to time by said Board. If any officer or member, or retired officer or member, shall die while in the service of the same or while so retired, and shall leave a widow, or if no widow, a child or children under the age of sixteen years, a sum not exceeding six hundred dollars a year, or such less sum as in the opinion of said Board the circumstances require, or the condition of the Fund warrant, shall be paid to such widow so long as she remains unmarried, or to such child or children until they respectively attain the age of sixteen years. In every such case said Board shall determine the circumstances thereof and order payment of the annuity to be made in such proportion to the parties entitled thereto, in case there be more than one, as they may deem just; but nothing herein contained shall render any payment of said annuity obligatory or chargeable as matter of legal right, and said Board may at any time order said annuity to be reduced or to cease.

SEC. 5. In case such Fund shall not be sufficient to pay the demands on it, such demands shall be audited and registered and paid in their order out of the Fund, as received. Said city and county shall never be liable for any deficiency in said Fund.

ARTICLE X.

Health Department.

CHAPTER I.

OF THE BOARD OF HEALTH.

SECTION 1. The Board of Health shall consist of three physicians in good and regular standing, who must be residents of said city and county for at least eight years next preceding their appointment.

They shall be appointed by the Mayor, and their term of office shall be for two years, commencing on the first Tuesday after the first day of January next succeeding their appointment. They shall serve without compensation.

CHAPTER II.

POWERS OF THE BOARD.

SECTION 1. Said Board shall have power to act in regard to all matters pertaining to public health, including the City and County Hospital,

County Jail, Alms House, Industrial School, Quarantine, and all public health institutions; the removal and disposal of the dead; the maintenance and operating of an ambulance service for the speedy removal of sick and needy persons; the registration of births, marriages and deaths; the registration of vital statistics in the said city and county, and to make such rules and regulations and such appointment of officers and employees as they may deem necessary for the proper carrying out and enforcement of all laws, ordinances and codes that may be prescribed for the government of said department, for the protection of the public health, and for the proper care and registration of such statistics.

SEC. 2. The said Board is hereby authorized and directed to prepare such rules and regulations as it shall deem to be required for the protection of the public health, for quarantine or other protection, and for securing the proper registration of births, marriages and deaths, and such other statistical information necessary for the efficient working of the department, with penalties for their violation, which rules and regulations shall be by them submitted to the Supervisors, and when approved by said Supervisors shall have and possess the same power and effect as other ordinances of said city and county, and shall be carried out and executed by said Board.

SEC. 3. The said Board of Health may appoint a Quarantine Officer, who must be a physician in good standing, and whose duties shall be defined by said Board; a superintendent and assistant superintendent of the City and County Hospital, who must have been residents of said city and county for at least five years, and must have been physicians in good standing for at least eight years next preceding their appointment. The superintendent or assistant superintendent must be on duty at the hospital at all hours of the day and night.

SEC. 4. The Board of Health shall also appoint two or more visiting physicians in good standing and two or more visiting surgeons in good standing, whose qualifications shall be the same as above, to the City and County Hospital, two of whom shall be nominated by the Faculty of the Medical

Department of the University of California, and two by the Faculty of the Cooper Medical College of this city. One-third of the wards of said Hospital, to be not less than five, shall be set apart for the use of the Medical Department of the University of California, and one-third, to be not less than five, shall be set apart for the use of the Cooper Medical College. Two wards of those remaining shall be set apart for the use of the Hahnemann Hospital College of San Francisco, and two for the California Medical College. Said four wards may be attended by physicians and surgeons nominated by their respective faculties. But no patient shall be assigned, against his or her wish, into a ward where he or she will not receive treatment from the school of medicine he or she prefers.

Provided, that the visiting physicians and surgeons so nominated shall not receive any pay for their services except the privilege of teaching students in the hospital wards, nor shall any visiting physician or surgeon appointed under this Charter receive any compensation for such services other than the privilege to teach students in the wards of the hospital; and

Provided, further, that all students matriculated at any legally chartered school of medicine in San Francisco shall have the privilege of attending upon all lectures and of witnessing all operations and shall have all other public privileges and advantages which may accrue to any student from the permission given to any physician or surgeon to practice, operate or lecture in the City and County Hospital aforesaid; and

Provided, further, that any regularly licensed physician or surgeon of the City and County of San Francisco, who may agree to render such free service, may be appointed if the members of the Faculties should refuse to nominate, or in case additional medical and surgical services should be required; and

Provided, further, that any regularly licensed physician may, upon proper permit given by the Mayor, attend any patient in the City and County Hospital who, upon admission to said Hospital, may request his services, and whom he is willing to serve without remuneration from city or patient. A special ward may be set aside for such cases.

Sec. 5. The Board of Health may appoint such internes to the City and County Hospital, not to exceed two for each ward thereof, as they may deem necessary. Said internes shall be appointed after a competitive examination by the Board of Health in any or all branches of medicine and surgery, Theory and Practice alone excepted. Such internes shall receive board and lodging free for their services. They shall be under the control and direction of the Superintendent of the Hospital, or in his absence, of the Assistant Superintendent, either of whom shall have power to remove any such interne for gross neglect of duty, or other good and sufficient cause, subject, however, to an appeal to, and final decision by, the Board of Health.

SEC. 6. The Board of Health shall also appoint one Steward, one Matron, one Apothecary, and one Engineer for the City and County Hospital, and such other employees as may be necessary.

SEC. 7. The visiting surgeons to the City and County Hospital shall have a general supervision over the City Receiving Hospital.

SEC. 8. The Board of Health shall also appoint a Resident Physician, and a Matron, and such other employees as may be necessary for the Alms House of said City and County.

They shall also appoint and prescribe the duties of one City Physician, and two or more Assistant City Physicians.

SEC. 9. They shall also appoint such other employees, health inspectors and medical attendants as may be deemed necessary in the Health Department, and in all the various institutions which are by law placed under their supervision. All appointments in the Health Department shall be made after a public competitive examination and no appointee shall be removed except for dishonesty, incompetency, neglect of duty, or other good and sufficient cause.

SECTION 10. The Assistant City Physicians shall be designated as Police Surgeons, and it shall be their duty to take charge of the Receiving Hospital of said City and County of San Francisco, and to make all autopsies required, together with such other duties as may be assigned them by the Board of Health.

SEC. 11. The Board of Health may appoint a Superintendent, who shall also be the Resident Physician of the Hospital for Infectious Diseases of the City and County of San Francisco.

CHAPTER III.

POWERS DEFINED.

SECTION 1. The said Board of Health shall have full power to enforce and carry out all ordinances, rules or regulations for the preservation of the public health, and for the registration of vital statistics, as are now or may be hereafter enacted by the Supervisors of the City and County of San Francisco; in the manner prescribed by this Charter, and to prohibit in said city any business or practice which said Board shall declare to be dangerous or detrimental to the public health. But no established business or the rights to property of any person shall be interfered with or prohibited, until the offender or offenders therewith charged, shall have been duly summoned by notice of not less than five days, to appear before said Board to show cause why such declaration or order of prohibition shall not be enforced against the said party or parties charged; nor until they shall have an opportunity to be heard. And upon the rendition of the decision of the said Board that said business or practice is detrimental to the public health, the said person or persons so charged shall have the right of appeal from such decision to the Superior Court of the City and County of San Francisco, upon petition reciting the said charges and decision, a copy of which petition shall be duly served upon the said Board within five days from the rendition of said decision. And said Superior Court shall proceed to a hearing and determination of such matter, which hearing shall be by trial of the issues embraced in the said petition, before said court, upon such day as the said court shall fix; and the decision of said Superior Court in said matter shall be final, and shall go into effect immediately thereafter. But no such appeal shall be had or taken, until a bond, to be approved by the court, shall have been duly filed with the court, conditioned in the sum of five hundred dollars, that the said appellant shall pay to the said Board all costs which may be awarded against such appellant or appellants, in case the said decision rendered by the said Board and appealed from shall be affirmed by final judgment.

Sec. 2. Every master or journeyman plumber carrying on his trade in the City and County of San Francisco, shall, under the rules and regulations prescribed by the said Board of Health, register his name and address at the said Department of Health, and it shall not be lawful for any person to carry on the trade of plumbing in said city and county unless his name and address be so registered. The drainage and plumbing of all buildings in said city and county, both public and private, shall be executed in accordance with plans previously approved in writing by said Board. Suitable drawings and descriptions of said plumbing and drainage shall in each case be submitted and placed on file in the Department of Health. The Board of Health is also authorized to receive and place on file drawings and descriptions of the plumbing and drainage of buildings heretofore erected, and they shall have power to condemn all or any portions of the plumbing which they may determine to be a menace to the health of the occupants thereof, subject to appeal as provided in Section 1 of this Chapter. Any court of record in said city and county shall have power at any time after the service of notice of the violation of any of the provisions of this section, and upon the affidavit of any member of the Board of Health to restrain by injunction order the further progress of any violation of the provisions of this section, or of any work upon or about the building or premises upon which the said violation exists, and no undertaking shall be required as a condition to the granting or issuing of any such injunction or by reason thereof. Any person violating any of the provisions of this section shall be deemed guilty of a misdemeanor.

Chapter IV.

OF THE HOSPITAL FOR CONTAGIOUS DISEASES.

Section 1. The Mayor, with the Board of Health and the Board of Public Works of the City and County of San Francisco, by and with the consent of the Supervisors, are hereby constituted a commission with power and authority, by this Charter, to select a site in or near the City and County of San Francisco, for the erection of a public hospital for the reception and treatment of persons suffering from infectious or contagious diseases. After such a site has been selected as aforesaid, it shall be purchased at a fair market value or leased by said Board of Health. The Auditor of the City of San Francisco is hereby authorized to include from year to year in his annual report, the sum or sums necessary for the purchase or lease of said site, and for the erection and maintenance of said hospital, and the sum or sums so reported shall be included in the annual tax levy of said city and county. After such site has been selected as aforesaid, either by purchase or lease, and whenever funds have been provided in the manner aforesaid, the said Board of Health is empowered by this Charter to take such property by purchase or lease in the name of the City and County of San Francisco, after the City Attorney shall have approved the validity of the title to the same. The management of said hospital shall be under the direction and control of the Board of Health of San Francisco. The said Board of Health shall make rules and regulations for the conduct and government of said hospital. It shall appoint all physicians necessary for said hospital, who shall be doctors of medicine, holding degrees from medical colleges in good standing. It shall appoint such employees, nurses and servants as may be necessary and determine their salaries, and shall regulate the scale of prices for those who are able to pay for admission and treatment. But no person having an infectious or contagious disease shall be refused admission to said hospital because of inability to pay. The Board of Health is hereby authorized to cause to be removed to this hospital any person or persons afflicted with contagious or infectious diseases, whose house and sanitary surroundings are not satisfactory to the said Board of Health. All moneys received from patients treated in this hospital shall be immediately paid into the Treasury.

ARTICLE XI.

Department of Elections.

CHAPTER I.

OF THE BOARD OF ELECTION COMMISSIONERS.

SECTION 1. The conduct, management and control of the registration of voters, and of the holding of elections, and of all matters pertaining to elections, in the City and County of San Francisco, shall be vested in and exercised by a Board of Election Commissioners, consisting of four members, who shall be appointed by the Mayor, and shall hold office for four years. Each member of said Board must be an elector, and must have been an actual resident of the city at least five years next preceding his appointment. Those first appointed must, immediately after their appointment, so classify themselves by lot, that one shall go out of office at the end of one year; one at the end of two years; one at the end of three years, and one at the end of four years. In making said appointments the Mayor shall not appoint more than two from the same political party, and said Board shall always be so composed that there shall never be at any one time more than two Commissioners from the same political party. No special election shall be called by said Board unless the same has been previously ordered by the Supervisors.

SEC. 2. No member of said Board shall, during his term of office, be a member of any convention, the purpose of which is to nominate candidates for office; or be eligible to any other public office during the term for which he shall have been appointed, or for one year thereafter; or act as officer of any election or primary election, or take part in any election except to deposit his vote and when acting as Election Commissioner, at which time he shall perform only such official duties as may be required of him by law and by this Charter.

SEC. 3. Said Commissioners shall organize within ten days after their appointment, by choosing one of their number President. In case of failure to agree, he shall be selected by lot, and shall hold office for one year and until his successor is elected. Said Board shall appoint a Registrar of Voters. He shall be the Secretary of the Board, and shall keep a record of its proceedings, and shall execute all orders, and enforce all rules and regulations adopted by the Board. He shall hold his office at the pleasure of the Board.

SEC. 4. Said Board may appoint a Deputy Registrar and such other clerical assistants as in its judgment may be necessary. The Board shall, by resolution adopted by a majority vote of all of its members and entered upon its minutes, designate the service to be rendered by such assistants, the rate of compensation, and the term for which they shall be employed. The time of employment so fixed shall not be extended except by like resolution of the Board, nor shall the salary so fixed before the employment, be increased in any case.

SEC. 5. Said Board shall, on or before the second Monday in June preceding each general election, divide the Assembly Districts of said city and county into election precincts, of which there shall be as many as shall be sufficient to make the number of votes polled at any one election precinct two hundred, as nearly as can be ascertained and arranged, using streets and avenues as boundaries. After said city and county shall have been so divided into precincts, the boundaries of any precinct may be changed by unanimous vote of said Board, so as to reduce the number of votes in any precinct to such number as said Board may consider best calculated to facilitate registration and the canvass of votes; *provided*, that if the use of voting machines shall hereafter be authorized by law, each precinct shall contain not more than one thousand votes.

SEC. 6. Said Board shall have all the powers, discharge all the duties, and be liable to all the obligations with respect to the registration of voters and other matters pertaining to elections, and election contests, in said city and county, now or hereafter belonging to, or imposed upon, the County Clerks of other counties of this State in their respective counties under the general laws thereof, so far as the same are not inconsistent with the provisions of this Charter.

SEC. 7. Said Board, in the third month preceding every general election, shall appoint the number of officers of precinct registration necessary for registration

purposes for each precinct. Said persons shall constitute the Board of Precinct Registration for said precinct, and shall serve for two years, unless sooner removed by the Board. In selecting officers of Precinct
Registration the Commissioners shall take care to select
as nearly as possible an equal number of persons of
different political faith and opinions to serve in each
precinct.

CHAPTER II.

OF THE REGISTRAR.

SECTION 1. The Registrar shall keep his office open for
business every day in the year (legal holidays other than
days of election excepted), from nine o'clock in the
forenoon till five o'clock in the afternoon, or during such
office hours as the Board may prescribe, and he shall
be in attendance thereat during said hours, except when
absent on official business. The Registrar, his Deputy and assistants, and also the Election Commissioners
and the members of Boards of Precinct Registration,
shall have power to administer oaths and affirmations in
all matters touching elections, the duties of their offices,
and the registration of voters or inquiry into their qualifications.

SEC. 2: The Registrar shall keep in his office an
alphabetical list of all deaths of adult males, occurring
in said city and county, as well as of the deaths of such
resident citizens of said city and county as may come to
his knowledge, who have died elsewhere. He shall also
keep a list of all removals from said city and county,
or changes of residence therein, so far as he can learn
the same, and of commitments to prisons and insane
asylums, with time and place, as well as such other
information as shall be useful. It shall be the duty of
all Public Officers, on demand, to furnish to said Registrar certified statements of such facts, within their
knowledge, as pertain to his duties.

SEC. 3. The Registrar, under and subject to the
rules of the Board, must take charge of the business of
placing the Election Officers, and when it is too late to
call the Board together to fill vacancies, may select and
appoint Election Officers for said purpose, from a list of
substitutes selected by said Board. Should any Election
Officer fail to appear at the opening of any election, or

at any time during the progress thereof, the officers in attendance may, subject to such rules as the Board may prescribe, fill the vacancy by appointing any competent citizen who is a registered elector of the precinct. In all cases in filling a vacancy the appointee shall be taken from the same political party as that of the person whose place is to be filled.

SEC. 4. The Registrar shall obtain from the Assessment Book and registers of voters of said city and county the names of the resident citizens possessing the necessary qualifications to act as Officers and Clerks of Election, taking care to select persons of good character, and have their names placed in a book, so as readily to refer to their places of residence and the precincts in which they vote. Said Board shall select from the book so prepared, all Election Officers provided for by law or by this Charter for said city and county, and shall appoint them for their respective places. They must be electors of said city and county, and able to read, write and speak the English language. In selecting such officers the Board must select, as nearly as possible, an equal number of persons of different political faith and opinions to serve at each precinct. The persons so selected must be residents of the precinct for which they are appointed.

CHAPTER III.

OF ELECTION OFFICERS.

SECTION 1. It is hereby made the duty of any and all voters in said city and county to serve as officers of election, and clerks, when required so to do under the provisions of this Article. The Inspectors shall receive as compensation for their services not more than two dollars a day when actually employed. The Board may provide for the compensation of clerks for matters requiring special skill and qualifications, such sum as may be necessary to secure such services, but not to exceed four dollars a day for any one clerk. No person holding any office or employment under the United States, the State of California, or said City and County, or any of its Departments, shall be eligible to, or allowed to serve as, an election or registration officer, or clerk, or in any manner whatsoever at an election.

SEC. 2. Each person appointed an officer of election shall be notified in writing by the Registrar of his appointment. Such notice must have printed thereon a copy of this section, and may be served by mail. Such person must, within the time fixed in the notice, which shall not be less than five days, appear before the Board and be examined as to his qualifications and fitness and shall serve as such officer for the term of two years from the date of his appointment, unless excused or dismissed by the Board; and in case of neglect or refusal to comply with the above mentioned requirements, or to serve, or act, shall be liable to a penalty of one hundred dollars, recoverable by civil action in any court of competent jurisdiction, in the name of said City and County, which, when collected, shall be paid into the Treasury. Failure on the part of any such person to comply with any of the requirements herein, preliminary to receiving his certificate of appointment or to attend on any day of registration, or revision, or examination of registration, or the day of any election during said term, unless prevented by sickness, or other sufficient cause (the burden of proof of which shall be upon the delinquent), shall be deemed a refusal within the meaning of this section.

SEC. 3. The persons so appointed officers of election shall each take and subscribe and file with the Registrar, before acting as such, and within ten days from the date of notice of appointment the following oath of office: " I, —————, residing at —————, do solemnly swear (or affirm) that I will support the Constitution of the United States, and of the State of California, and that I will faithfully discharge the duties of ————— of election for the City and County of San Francisco, in Election Precinct ————— of Assembly District —————, according to the best of my ability; that I am a citizen and qualified voter of the State of California and resident of said precinct, and not a candidate for office to be voted for by the electors of the precinct for which I am appointed, and that I do not hold any office or employment under the United States, the State of California, the City and County of San Francisco, or any Department thereof; and that I have not made any bet of money or property of any kind on the result of the election about to be held."

No payment shall be made to any election officer who shall not have taken, subscribed and filed such oath, or affirmation, or who shall not during his period of service have fully complied with the requirements of law relating to his duties, and have properly completed said service.

Sec. 4. Each person so appointed and qualified shall receive a certificate of appointment from the Registrar in such form as may be prescribed by the Board of Election Commissioners. It shall specify the Assembly District and Precinct for which he is appointed and the date of the expiration of his term of office. He may be removed at any time by said Board for want of any of the requisite qualifications. When any officer or clerk is appointed to fill a vacancy, that fact shall be stated in his certificate of appointment, and he shall hold office only for the unexpired term. No officer or clerk shall be transferred from one election precinct to another after his appointment.

CHAPTER IV.

OF REGISTRATION.

Section 1. The Registration of voters in said city and county shall be by election precincts. The provisions of the Political Code, as they now are or may hereafter be, as to making and keeping the Great Register, and the manner of entering names therein, and the substance and contents of said entries, and the alterations, changes, and cancellation thereof, as well as the proceedings and proofs to enable voters to be registered in said Great Register, and all matters relating thereto, so far as the same are not inconsistent with the provisions of this Charter, shall be applicable to the precinct Registers of said city and county. Said Precinct Registers shall be used at all elections, and no person shall vote at any election unless he is legally registered upon the Precinct Register of the precinct in which he is a qualified voter.

Sec. 2. The registration of voters as herein provided, shall take place previous to each general election, and an elector properly registered may, without again being registered, if he has not changed his residence, vote at the general election next ensuing after his regis-

12

tration, and at all special elections between said general election and the next general election, but not afterwards, unless re-registered according to law.

SEC. 3. The Board of Election Commissioners shall cause to be prepared books for the registration of voters in manner hereinafter provided. Said books shall be called Precinct Registers, and shall be so arranged as to admit of the entering, under the name of each street or avenue in each election precinct, and the number of each dwelling on any such street or avenue, if there be a number thereto, and if there be no number, under such other definite description of the location of the dwelling-place as shall enable it to be readily ascertained, found and located, of the names of all electors resident in each dwelling in each of said precincts who shall apply for registration. Said Registers shall be ruled in parallel columns, in which, opposite to and against the name of every applicant, shall be entered words and figures of the character hereinafter provided in this article, and each of said Registers shall be of such size as to contain not less than three hundred names, and so prepared that it may be used at each election in said city and county until such time as is provided for the succeeding general registration, and shall be of such form and appearance as shall be established by the Registrar of Voters, after submission to and approval by the Board of Election Commissioners.

To each precinct Register shall be prefixed an alphabetical index of all the names contained therein, and opposite to each name shall be set its register number.

SEC. 4. The following oath or affirmation shall be administered to all persons who apply for registration: "You do solemnly swear [or affirm] that you will fully and truly answer all such questions as shall be put to you touching your place of residence, name, place of birth, your qualifications as an elector, and your right as such to register and vote."

SEC. 5. The Board of Precinct Registration shall examine each applicant as to his qualifications as an elector, and shall immediately, in the presence of the applicant, enter in the said Register, and in a duplicate thereof, the statements and facts below set forth in manner following, namely:

First—In the column headed " Residence," the name

and number of the street, avenue, or other location of the dwelling, if there be a number, but if there be not a number, such clear and definite description of the place of said dwelling as will enable it to be readily ascertained, fixed and determined; and, if there be more than one house at the number given by the applicant as his place of residence, in which of said houses he resides, or if there be more than one family residing in said house, or if the place of his residence be a hotel, boarding house or lodging house, then in the column headed "Floor of House," the floor on which he resides, and in the column headed "Number and Location of Room," the number and location of the room or rooms occupied by him.

Second—In the column headed "Names," the name of the applicant, giving the surname and Christian name in full. The names of all the voters residing in the same dwelling shall follow each other and shall refer to the house and street, number or other description, as provided, of the dwelling.

Third—In the column headed "Sworn," the word "Yes" or "No" as the fact shall be.

Fourth—In the column headed "Nativity," the state or country, as the fact shall be stated by the applicant.

Fifth—In the column headed "Age," the age of the applicant, rejecting fractions of the year.

Sixth—In the column headed "Color," the word "White" or "Colored" as the fact is.

Seventh—In the column headed "Occupation," the business or profession of the applicant.

Eighth—In the subdivisions of the general column headed "Term of Residence," the period by months or years stated by the applicant in response to the inquiries made concerning the subject of each of said subdivisions.

Ninth—In the subdivisions of the general column headed "Naturalization," in cases where the applicant claims to be a naturalized citizen, in the subdivision whether he claims by the naturalization of his father, "Yes" or "No," as the case may be, and in the other subdivisions, the time and place of naturalization, the name of the Court where naturalized, (if the applicant know such name), whether or not the certificate is lost, and the date of the papers of naturalization, as the same shall appear by the evidence of citizenship submitted or presented by the applicant.

Tenth—In the column headed "Qualified Voter," the word "Yes" or "No," as the fact shall appear and be determined by a majority of the Board of Precinct Registration ; but they must designate as a qualified voter any person who, being otherwise qualified, is not of age at the time of making such application, if such applicant will be of the age of twenty-one years prior to or on the day of election immediately following such time of applying.

Eleventh—In the column of "Date of Application," the month, day and year when the applicant presented himself and was adjudged a qualified voter of the election precinct.

Twelfth—In the column "Challenge," "Yes" or "No," according to the fact, whether challenged or not.

Thirteenth—In the column "Signature of the Voter," the applicant shall sign his name, if he be able to write, and if he be not, his name shall be written for him, and the fact attested in the margin by the signature of the Chairman of the Board of Precinct Registration.

Sec. 6. The registration of voters, and all proceedings connected therewith, shall be public, and citizens shall have free ingress and egress to and from the place where the same is being done.

CHAPTER V.

OF BOARDS OF PRECINCT REGISTRATION.

Section 1. The Board of Election Commissioners shall procure a suitable room or place, which shall have an area of not less than two hundred square feet, in each election precinct for the sittings of the Boards of Precinct Registration. In each election precinct such place shall be in the most public, orderly and convenient portion of the precinct, and no building or part of building shall be designated or used as a place of registry or polling place in which, or any part of which, spirituous or intoxicating liquors are sold; and no place shall be designated or used for any such purpose unless the same is well lighted. Places so selected for precinct registration may be used as polling places, except at such time when the law requires the use of election booths, in which case they shall be provided and erected by said Board.

SEC. 2. Said Boards of Precinct Registration shall meet in the places provided in their respective precincts for such purpose, commencing sixty days before the day of election, and shall sit in open session from eight o'clock in the forenoon until ten o'clock in the afternoon of each day for six days next thereafter (legal holidays excepted), to receive and act upon applications for registration on the part of the voters of said precinct. They shall organize by electing one of their number Chairman. In case of a failure to so organize within one hour after the time fixed for their meeting, the Chairman shall be selected by them by lot. They shall receive the applications for registration of such residents of their several election precincts as then are, or on the day of election next following the day of making such application, would be, entitled to vote therein, and who shall personally apply, with proper evidence of their rights.

SEC. 3. The Registrar shall, under the direction of the said Commissioners, furnish said Boards of Precinct Registration with blanks, stationery, and all other matters and things necessary to enable them to conveniently and speedily perform their duties. He shall also give such Boards his assistance and advice in organizing and conducting registration and other matters required of them by law, and shall visit said Boards while engaged in said duty, and see that said proceedings are conducted according to law, and that the Registers are made in due form. The public shall be allowed free access to the Precinct Registers.

SEC. 4. The Boards of Precinct Registration shall keep the several Precinct Registers for three days after the expiration of the time prescribed for their sitting for registration, during which time they shall make diligent examination and inquiry by a house to house canvass as to the right of the respective voters who have been registered on said Precinct Registers to such registration, and shall, in all doubtful cases, certify said doubt, with the reasons therefor, to the Board of Election Commissioners for their action. All persons who have been refused registration by the Registrar, or by the Precinct Board, may appeal to the Board of Election Commissioners, who shall hear and determine the same in a summary manner, so as not to delay the completion of the Registers.

Sec. 5. When each Board of Precinct Registration has completed the examination and inquiry required in the preceding section, it shall certify the Precinct Register with said index and the duplicate thereof as is hereinafter provided, and deliver the same to the Registrar. Said delivery shall be made not later than four full days after the cessation of its sitting for registration. The said Board shall at the same time prepare and duly certify a separate and distinct list, showing the names of all persons concerning whose right to registration it is in doubt, together with the grounds and reasons for such doubt. Such list and certificate shall be delivered to the Registrar at the same time with the Precinct Register. Proper blanks shall be prepared and furnished by the Registrar for the purpose of making the return of doubtful names on the Registers, and also blank certificates and all other necessary things for such purpose.

Sec. 6. The certificate to be attached to the Precinct Register shall be substantially in the following form, to wit: " We the undersigned, officers of Election, forming the Board of Precinct Registration for the...................... Precinct of the........ Assembly District in the City and County of San Francisco, do jointly and severally certify that on the ...... day of........................, 18...., we met and organized as such Board, at the place appointed by law for the holding thereof in said precinct. We further certify that we sat as a Board of Precinct Registration at said place, from the .... day of ...., till the .... day of........... 18....., and have admitted to registration (showing number) citizens, whose names and other matters of qualification will appear upon the foregoing register, and that the whole number of qualified voters upon said Register is (number.) We further certify that we have made a house to house canvass and have examined and inquired into said list to the best of our ability, and have noted all doubtful registration thereon.

"Dated, ..., 18....

"(Signed):   ——— ———

"(Signed):   ——— ———

"(Signed):   ——— ———

"(Signed):   ——— ——— "

SEC. 7. The certificate to be annexed to the list of doubtful names shall be substantially in the following form, to wit: " We, the undersigned, composing the Board of Precinct Registration, for the............. Precinct of the................Assembly District in the City and County of San Francisco, hereby certify that the accompanying list shows all the names and other matters of qualification of voters upon the Precinct Register for said precinct, about whose right to registration we entertain a reasonable doubt, together with a statement of the cause or grounds for such doubt.

"Dated,....................., 18....

"(Signed):   ——— ———

"(Signed):   ——— ———

"(Signed):   ——— ———

"(Signed):   ——— ——— "

SEC. 8. Any member of such Precinct Boards of Registration, who shall fail to perform any of the duties required of him, or who shall make any false returns or statement, or who shall violate any of the provisions of this Article, shall be guilty of a misdemeanor, where the offense is not otherwise specified.

CHAPTER VI.

OF THE PRECINCT REGISTERS.

SECTION 1. The Registrar shall forthwith notify all persons whose right to registration is certified as doubtful, of said fact, and also in cases where the Registrar has reason to believe that persons have been illegally registered, and shall cite them before the Board of Election Commissioners. He shall forthwith send a written or printed notice to such person, directing the same to him at his address as found in said Precinct Register, requiring such person to show cause before the Board of Election Commissioners, at a day to be named in said notice, why said Board should not cancel said name. If such person fail for five days after the day fixed for the hearing, to appear and establsh the legality of his registration, and if the Registrar certify that notice in accordance herewith has been given, the Board shall, if it appears to its satisfaction that such name is illegally upon the Precinct Register, make and enter an order directing the Registrar to cancel such registration.

Sec. 2. Fifty-four days before a general election all registration by Boards of Precinct Registration shall cease, and the Precinct Registers, as they stand, shall be the Precinct Registers for said ensuing election and until the next general election, subject only to changes in the following cases:

First—Any name that for any reason is illegally on any Precinct Register shall be cancelled.

Second—Any name that has once been legally on the Precinct Register, so as to entitle the person to vote at said ensuing election, and which has been by fraud, mistake or otherwise improperly removed or cancelled, may be restored, on satisfactory evidence thereof, by order of the Board of Election Commissioners.

Third—Any voter entitled to have his name upon the Precinct Register under the terms of the last preceding subdivision, may have the same placed upon the supplemental list hereinafter provided for, within ten days from the time herein provided for the cessation of registration. Any person who does not so apply within said time shall not be registered on the Precinct Register for said election.

Sec. 3. The Board of Election Commissioners shall at or about the time of the commencement of any registration in said City and County, contract for the printing in type, when completed, of said Precinct Registers and indexes. The contract or contracts shall require the printing of not more than two hundred copies of each Precinct Register, and that the same be completed within twelve days after the receipt of the duplicate of each Precinct register by the Registrar. The printing shall be awarded to the bidder making the lowest bid for each name registered, counting said indexes as a part of the Register, and counting each name only once. Said Board may reject any and all bids.

Sec. 4. As soon as the Registrar shall receive the

Precinct Registers from the Boards of Precinct Registration, he shall proceed immediately to ascertain the correctness of said Precinct Registers, and after completion shall turn them over to the Board of Election Commissioners, who shall order the same printed. The Registrar and his assistants shall supervise said printing and see that all contracts with reference thereto are faithfully performed. Copies of said Registers when printed shall be immediately posted in the office of the Board. The Registrar shall furnish ten copies of each of said Precinct Registers or more, at the discretion of the Board to the authorized representatives of every political party applying to him for the same. The Precinct Registers shall be distributed, as early as possible, and at least fifteen days before the day of election, after which no changes shall be made, excepting any person whose term of residence in the Precinct shall meet the requirements of the law on the day when registration ceases, or who through failure in that requirement has been denied registration, may have his name placed on the register of his Precinct by and with the approval of the Board of Election Commissioners after proper consideration of each case submitted. All cancellations or additions to the Registers shall be made by the Registrar, subject to the approval of the Board of Election Commissioners. All names added to the Precinct Registers under the provisions of this section shall be included in a Supplemental Precinct Register, which shall be printed and distributed as soon as possible after completion.

Sec. 5. Not less than five days before the day fixed for the first sitting of the Boards of Precinct Registration the Registrar shall cause an advertisement to be printed in four daily newspapers of general circulation, published in said city and county, one of which shall be the official newspaper, giving notice to the voters of said city and county of the time when the registration of voters on the Precinct Registers will expire, and inviting them to apply within said time for registration at the place of meeting of said Boards (which shall be named), under penalty of being debarred the privilege of voting at such election. Such notice shall specify the days upon which the precinct registration by said Boards shall commence and end, and shall be published daily until the termination of the sittings of said Boards for registration. Such notice shall also contain the names of the officers comprising the Boards of Precinct Registration.

CHAPTER VII.

OF ELECTIONS AND CANVASS OF VOTES.

SECTION 1. The Boards of Precinct Registration shall constitute the Boards of Election for their several precincts, and as such shall receive and deposit in the several ballot-boxes the ballots of those presenting themselves in their proper precincts who are entitled to vote. They shall keep the poll and tally lists prescribed by law, and shall exercise all the powers and be subject to all the duties prescribed by law, including such as may hereafter be imposed upon them by the adoption of voting machines, except so far as the same may be inconsistent with the provisions of this Charter.

SEC. 2. At every election each political party shall have the right to designate, and keep a challenger at each place of registration and voting, who shall be assigned such position as will enable him to see each person as he offers to register or vote, and who shall be protected in the discharge of his duty by the officers of election and the police. Any political party may remove any challenger appointed by it, and may appoint another in his place who shall have the like authority as was conferred by the original appointment.

SEC. 3. No certificate of the Registrar or of any other officer shall ever be taken as the basis of a right to vote. The Register shall be the only evidence of the right to vote, and no person whose name is not thereon shall be allowed to vote.

SEC. 4. Any person applying to register, or who, being registered, offers to vote, may, on any day of registration or of election, be challenged by any qualified elector of said city and county, and either of the said officers may, and one of them shall, at any authorized meeting of the Board of Precinct Registration, or of the Board of Election, administer to any person so challenged, the oath or oaths provided by law to test the qualification of challenged electors, and shall also administer to any elector of the election precinct who may be offered as a witness to prove the qualification of any person claiming the right to be registered, or to vote, the following oath: "You do swear (or affirm) that you are a voter of this election precinct, that you will fully and truly answer all such questions as shall be put to you touching the place of residence and other qualifications as a voter of the person (name to be given) now claiming the right to be registered (or to vote) in this precinct?"

SEC. 5. For all powers, authority and duties herein prescribed for and conferred upon, and all action required of, Boards of Precinct Registration or Boards of Election, save where such authority or action is specifically allowed to any of said Officers, the concurrence or assent of a majority of all the Officers of Election in any election precinct, must in all cases be obtained.

SEC. 6. The Officers of Election in each election precinct, while discharging any of the duties imposed upon them shall have full authority to preserve order and enforce obedience to their lawful commands at and around the place of registration or election; to keep the access to such place open and unobstructed; to prevent and suppress riots, tumults, violence, disorder and all other practices tending to the intimidation or obstruction of voters, or the disturbance or interruption of the work of registration or voting, or tending to the obstruction of the performance by them of any of their duties, and to protect the voters and challengers from intimidation or violence, and the registers and poll lists, boxes and ballots from violence and fraud, and shall appoint or deputize, if necessary, one or more persons to communicate their orders and directions, and to assist in the enforcement thereof.

SEC. 7. The Board of Election Commissioners may, prior to any election, appoint from each precinct such additional Officers and Clerks as they may deem necessary. When such appointments are made, the additional Officers, with the original Officers, shall canvass the vote for such precinct, and shall from and after the closing of the polls, constitute the Board of Election of such precinct, the members relieving each other in the duty of canvassing the ballots, which may be conducted by at least half of the entire number; but the certificates must be signed by at least two-thirds of the whole number.

SEC. 8. Said additional Officers and Clerks shall be

as nearly as possible divided equally in number as to their political faith and opinions. They shall possess the other qualifications required by this Article, and shall be in all respects named, selected, notified, examined, appointed, commissioned, and sworn, as hereinbefore provided.

They shall hold office during the counting of the vote, and shall receive the same compensation a day as the other Officers and Clerks herein provided for. If any one of said additional Officers or Clerks is not present at the precinct at the closing of the polls the Precinct Board of Election must fill the vacancy by the appointment of some suitable person of the same political faith and opinions and qualifications as the absent person.

SEC. 9. The polls must be opened at sunrise of the day of election and kept open continously until five o'clock in the afternoon of the same day, when they shall be closed.

SEC. 10. As soon as the polls of an election are closed the Officers in their several election precincts shall immediately, and at the place of the polls, proceed to canvass the votes. Such canvass shall be made in the manner required by the laws of the State, shall be public, and shall not be adjourned or postponed until it shall have been fully completed. No vote shall be received, nor shall any ballot be counted or canvassed, nor shall any statement of votes, announcement, or proclamation be made at any time when the main entrance to the room in which the election is held shall be closed in such a manner as to prevent ingress or egress; but the said Board may station one or more officers at such entrance to exclude disorderly and improper persons; nor shall any such duties be performed unless at least six persons, if so many claim that privilege, are allowed to be present, and so near that they can see whether the duties of the said Officers are faithfully performed. Each political party shall be entitled to designate and keep watchers present during the canvass, provided that at no time shall there be in attendance more than two watchers from any one party. When the canvass is completed, the returns shall be made in the manner provided by law and immediately delivered to the Board of Election Commissioners.

SEC. 11. All provisions for carrying out the registration and election laws in said city and county shall be made by the Board of Election Commissioners, and demands on the Treasury authorized or allowed by it for such purposes shall be paid upon demands signed by the President and Secretary of said Board, and after being duly audited.

ARTICLE XII.

OF THE CIVIL SERVICE.

SECTION 1. It is hereby declared to be the intent and purpose of this Charter that the Government of the City and County of San Francisco and each and every department thereof shall be managed and conducted on business principles. The salaries and compensation of its clerks and employees shall be fixed and regulated from time to time at no higher rates than those paid for the rendition of similar services in commercial employments in said city and county. There shall be no discharge or removal of such clerks or employees in any of the departments of the city and county government, after their employment as hereinafter provided, for political reasons, or for any other reasons than for dishonesty, inefficiency, insubordination or habitual discourtesy to the public. To the end that efficiency and faithful service may be encouraged the salaries of all clerks and employees in all the departments of the city government hereinafter mentioned shall be fixed and regulated upon a graduated scale, by which such salaries shall be increased by length of service faithfully rendered.

SEC. 2. For the purpose of applying and carrying into practical effect the principles set forth in the preceding section, immediately upon the taking effect of this Charter the Mayor shall appoint three persons known by him to be devoted to the principles of Civil Service Reform and opposed to the system of rewarding political party services by political appointment, who shall constitute and be known as the Civil Service Commissioners, one for three years, one for two years, and one for one year from the time of appointment, and until after their respective successors are appointed and qualified; and in every year thereafter the Mayor shall,

in like manner, appoint one person as the successor of
the commissioner whose term shall expire in that year,
to serve as such commissioner for three years, and until
his successor is appointed and qualified. Two commissioners shall constitute a quorum. All appointments to
said commission, both original and to fill vacancies,
shall be so made that not more than two members shall
at the time of any appointment be members of the
same political party. Said commissioners shall hold
no other public office or employment. Each commissioner, before entering upon the duties of his office,
shall take the oath prescribed by the Constitution of the
State.

SEC. 3. The Mayor shall remove any Commissioner
for incompetence, neglect of duty, or malfeasance in
office, but for no other cause. The Mayor shall report
in writing any such removal to the Supervisors with his
reasons therefor. Any vacancy in the office of Commissioner shall be filled by appointment by the Mayor.

SEC. 4. Said Commission shall classify all the offices
and places of employment mentioned in section twelve
of this Article with reference to the examinations herein
provided for. The offices and places so classified by
the Commission shall constitute the classified civil service of said city and county; and no appointment to
any such offices or places shall be made except under
and according to the rules hereinafter mentioned.

SEC. 5. Said Commission shall make rules to carry
out the purposes of this Article and for examinations
and appointments in accordance with its provisions, and
the Commission may, from time to time, make changes
in the original rules.

SEC. 6. All rules made as hereinbefore provided, and
all changes therein, shall be printed for distribution by
said Commission; and the Commission shall give notice
of the place or places where said rules may be obtained,
by publication in the official paper, and in each said
publications shall be specified the date, not less than
thirty days subsequent to the date of such publication,
when said rules shall go into operation.

SEC. 7. All applicants for offices or places in said
classified service, shall be subjected to examination,
which shall be public, competitive and free to all
citizens of the United States, with specified limita-

tions as to residence, age, health, habits and moral character. Such examinations shall be practical in their character and shall relate to those matters which will fairly test the relative capacity of the persons examined to discharge the duties of the positions to which they seek to be appointed, and shall include tests of physical qualifications and health, and, when appropriate, of manual skill. No question in any examination shall relate to political or religious opinions or affiliations. The Commission shall control all examinations, and may, whenever an examination is to take place, designate a suitable number of persons, either in or not in the official service of the city, to be Examiners, and it shall be the duty of such Examiners, and if in the service it shall be a part of their official duty, without extra compensation to conduct such examinations as the Commission may direct, and make return or report thereof to said Commission, and the Commission may at any time substitute any other person, whether or not in such service, in the place of any one so selected; and the Commission may themselves at any time act as such Examiners, and without appointing Examiners. The Examiners at any examination shall not all be members of the same political party.

Sec. 8. Notice of the time, place, and general scope of every examination shall be given by the Commission by publication, for four weeks preceding such examination, in the official paper, and such notice shall also be posted by said Commission in a conspicuous place at the City Hall and in their office four weeks before such examination.

Sec. 9. From the returns or reports of the Examiners, or from the examinations made by the Commission, the Commission shall prepare a register for each grade or class of position in the classified service of the city, of the persons whose general average standing upon examination for such grade or class is not less than the minimum fixed by the rules of said Commission, and who are otherwise eligible; and such persons shall take rank upon the register as candidates in the order of their relative excellence as determined by examination, without reference to priority at time of examination. When the examinations are oral they must be open to the public, and, when written, the examination papers of each application shall be placed on file and kept in the office of the Commission and constitute public records open to the inspection of any citizen.

SEC. 10. The Commission shall by its rules provide for promotions in such classified service on the basis of ascertained merit and seniority in service and examination, and shall provide in all cases where it is practicable that vacancies shall be filled by promotion. All examinations for promotion shall be competitive among such members of the next lower rank as desire to submit themselves to such examination; and it shall be the duty of the Commission to submit to the appointing power the names of not more than three applicants for each promotion having the highest rating; but in fixing said rating, a uniform allowance of credits to be stated at the time of the announcement of said examination shall be made for each year of past service. The method of examination and the rules governing the same, and the method of certifying, shall be the same as provided for applicants for original appointment.

SEC. 11. The head of the department or office in which a position classified under this Article is to be filled shall notify said Commission of that fact, and said Commission shall certify to such officer the name and address of one or more candidates, not exceeding three, standing highest upon the register for the class or grade to which said position belongs, except that in cases where a choice by competition is impracticable, said Commission may provide by its rules that the selections shall be made by lot from among those candidates proved fit by examination. In making such certification sex shall be disregarded except when some statute, the rules of said Commission, or the appointing power, specifies sex. Said appointing officer shall notify said Commission of each position to be filled separately, and shall fill such place from the names certified to him by said Commission therefor. One of the candidates thus certified shall thereupon be appointed by said head of such department or office and employed on probation for a period to be fixed by said rules. Each candidate, unless he shall be sooner appointed or otherwise lawfully cease to be a candidate, shall be certified for appointment in the grade or class for which he is eligible, not less than three times, and no candidate shall lose his place on the register by certification and rejection, except that said Commission may strike off names of candidates from the register after they have remained thereon more than two years. At or before the expiration of the period of probation, the head of the department, or office in which a candidate is employed, may discharge him upon assigning in writing his reasons therefore to said Commission. If he is not then discharged his appointment shall be deemed complete. To prevent the stoppage of public business or to meet extraordinary exigencies, the head of any department or office may, under such regulations as the Commission may by its rules precribe, make temporary appointments in the classified civil service, to remain in force not exceeding sixty days, and only until regular appointments under the provisions of this Article can be made.

SEC. 12. The provisions of this Article shall apply to the following offices and Departments of the city and county, to-wit: the County Clerk, the Assessor, the Tax Collector, the Sheriff, the Auditor, the Recorder, the Clerks of the Justices' Court, the Board of Public Works, the Police Department, the Fire Department and the Board of Election Commissioners. *Provided,* that the following deputies, clerks and employees in said offices and Departments shall be exempted therefrom, to wit: the Chief Deputy of the County Clerk, the Chief Deputy of the Assessor, the Chief Deputy and Cashier of the Tax Collector, the Under Sheriff and Chief Bookkeeper of the Sheriff, the Deputy Auditor, the Chief Deputy of the Recorder, the Superintendent of Public Works, the City Engineer and the Architect of the Board of Public Works, the Registrar of the Board of Election Commissioners, the Chief of Police, Chief Engineer of the Fire Department, and all clerks, laborers and employees in said offices and Departments not permanently employed at monthly salaries. All officers, Boards and heads of departments vested in this Charter with the power to appoint deputies, clerks, or employees in any of the offices or departments of the city and county government herein mentioned shall make such appointments in conformity with the rules and provisions prescribed by this Article.

SEC. 13. No officer or employee in the classified civil

13

service of the city who shall have been appointed under said rules, and after said examination, shall be removed or discharged except for cause, upon written charges, and after an opportunity to be heard in his own defense. Such charges shall be publicly investigated by or before said Civil Service Commission, or by or before some officer or board appointed by said Commission to conduct such investigation. The finding and decision of such Commission, or investigating officer or board, when approved by such Commission, shall be certified to the appointing officer, and shall be forthwith enforced by such officer. Nothing in this Article shall limit the power of any officer to suspend a subordinate for a reasonable period, not exceeding thirty days. In the course of an investigation of charges each member of the Commission and of any board so appointed by it, and any officer so appointed, shall have the power to administer oaths, and shall have power to secure by its subpœna both the attendance and testimony of witnesses, and the production of books and papers relevant to such investigation. No one shall be excused from testifying at such investigation for any cause.

SEC. 14. Immediate notice in writing shall be given by the appointing power, to said Commission, of all appointments, permanent or temporary, made in such classified civil service, and of all transfers, promotions, resignations or vacancies from any cause in such service, and of the date thereof; and a record of the same shall be kept by said Commission. When any office or place of employment is created or abolished, or the compensation attached thereto altered, the officer or board making such change shall immediately report in writing to said commission.

SEC. 15. The Commission shall investigate the enforcement of this Article and of its rules, and the action of the Examiners herein provided for, and the conduct and action of the appointees in the classified service in the city, and may inquire as to the nature, tenure, and compensation of all offices and places of the public service thereof. In the course of such investigations each commissioner shall have the power to administer oaths, and said Commission shall have power to, by its subpœna, compel both the attendance and testimony of witnesses and the production of books and papers relevant to such investigations.

SEC. 16. Said Commission shall, on or before the 15th day of January in each year, make to the Mayor for transmission to the Supervisors a report showing its own action, the rules in force, the practical effects thereof, and suggestions it may approve for the more effectual accomplishment of the purposes of this article. The Mayor may require a report from said Commission at any other time.

SEC. 17. Said Commission shall employ a Chief Examiner, whose duty it shall be, under the direction of the Commission, to superintend any examinations held in the city under this Article, and who shall perform such other duties as the Commission shall prescribe. The Chief Examiner shall be *ex-officio* Secretary of said Commission. Under the direction of such Commission he, as such Secretary, shall keep minutes of its proceedings, preserve all reports made to it, keep a record of all examinations held under its direction, and perform such other duties as the Commission shall prescribe.

SEC. 18. All officers of said city and county shall aid said commissioners in all proper ways in carrying out the provisions of this chapter.

SEC. 19. The Supervisors shall furnish said commissioners with suitable offices, and shall provide office furniture, books, stationery, blanks, heat and light, and are authorized and required to pay such other expenses as may be necessarily incurred by said commissioners in carrying out the provisions of this Article.

SEC. 20. No person or officer shall willfully and corruptly, by himself or in co-operation with one or more other persons defeat, deceive, or obstruct any person in respect to his or her right of examination, or corruptly or falsely mark, grade, estimate, or report upon the examination or proper standing of any person examined hereunder, or aid in so doing; or willfully or corruptly make any false representations concerning the same, or concerning the person examined; or willfully or corruptly furnish to any person any special or secret information for the purpose of either improving or injuring the prospects or chances of any person so examined or to be examined, being appointed, employed or promoted.

SEC. 21. No applicant for appointment in said classified civil service, either directly or indirectly, shall pay, or promise to pay, any money or other valuable thing to any person whatever for or on account of his appointment or proposed appointment, and no other officer or employee shall pay or promise to pay, either directly or indirectly, any person any money or other valuable thing whatever for or on account of his promotion.

SEC. 22. No accounting or auditing officer shall allow the claim of any public officer for services of any deputy or other person employed in the public service in violation of the provisions of this Article.

SEC. 23. The Commission shall certify to the Auditor all appointments to offices and places in the classified civil service, and all vacancies occurring therein, whether by dismissal, resignation, or death and all findings made or approved by the Commission under the provisions of section thirteen of this Article, that a person shall be discharged from the classified civil service.

SEC. 24. The Auditor shall not approve or pay any salary or wages to any person for services as an officer or employee of such city before the appointment of such person to the classified civil service has been certified by the Commission, nor after the vacation of such person's appointment shall have been so certified, nor after the Commission shall have certified to the Auditor a finding made or approved by it under section thirteen of this Article that such person shall be discharged from the classified civil service.

SEC. 25. Any person who shall be served with a subpœna to appear and testify, or to produce books and papers, issued by the Commission or by any Commissioner, or by any board of persons acting under the orders of the Commission in the course of an investigation conducted either under the provisions of Section 13 or Section 15 of this Article, and who shall refuse or neglect to appear or to testify, or to produce books and papers relevant to said investigation, as commanded in such subpœna, shall be guilty of a misdemeanor. The fees of witnesses for attendance and travel shall be the same as the fees of witnesses before the Superior Court, and shall be paid from the appropriation for the expenses of the Commission. Any court, or any Judge thereof, upon application of such commissioner, or officer, or board, may, in his discretion, compel the attendance of witnesses, the production of books and papers, and the giving of testimony before the commission or before any such commissioner, investigating board, or officer, by attachment for contempt or otherwise, in the same manner as the production of evidence may be compelled before said court.

SEC. 26. Any person who shall willfully, or through culpable negligence violate any provision of this Article or any rule promulgated in accordance with the provisions thereof shall be guilty of a misdemeanor.

SEC. 27. If any person shall be convicted under the next preceding section, any public office which such person may hold shall, by force of such conviction, be rendered vacant, and such person shall be incapable of holding office for the period of five years from the date of such conviction.

SEC. 28. Prosecutions for violations of this Article shall be instituted by the District Attorney, or by the Commission acting through special counsel.

ARTICLE XIII.

Bonds and Salaries.

CHAPTER I.

OF BONDS.

SECTION 1. Officers of the city and county, before entering upon the discharge of their official duties, shall respectively give and execute to said city and county such official bonds as may be required by law, ordinance or this Charter. When the amount of any bond is not fixed by law or by this Charter, and power to fix the same is not herein conferred upon any Board or officer, it shall be fixed by an ordinance of the Supervisors. All bonds, excepting that of the Auditor, must be approved by the Mayor and Auditor. The bond of the Auditor must be approved by the Mayor. The approval of every official bond must be indorsed thereon, and signed by the officers approving the same, after examination of the sureties, as hereinafter provided. Upon the approval of a bond it must be recorded, at the expense of the party giving the same, in the office of the Recorder, in a book kept for that purpose, entitled

"Record of Official Bonds." The bond of the Auditor shall be filed and kept in the office of the County Clerk. The bonds of all other officers shall be filed and kept in the office of the Auditor.

SEC. 2. The following officers shall respectively execute to the City and County of San Francisco official bonds, with sureties, in the following sums, viz.:

Auditor, fifty thousand dollars.
Treasurer, one hundred and fifty thousand dollars.
Tax Collector, one hundred thousand dollars.
Assessor, fifty thousand dollars.
County Clerk, fifty thousand dollars.
Recorder, twenty thousand dollars.
Sheriff, one hundred thousand dollars.
Coroner, ten thousand dollars.
City Attorney, twenty thousand dollars.
District Attorney, twenty thousand dollars.
Public Administrator, fifty thousand dollars.
Superintendent of Public Schools, ten thousand dollars.
Each Commissioner of the Board of Public Works, twenty-five thousand dollars.
Clerk of the Board of Supervisors, ten thousand dollars.
Each Member of the Supervisors, ten thousand dollars.
Each School Director, ten thousand dollars.
Each Justice of the Peace, five thousand dollars.
Each Fire Commissioner, ten thousand dollars.
Each Police Commissioner, ten thousand dollars.
Each Election Commissioner, ten thousand dollars.
Property Clerk of Police Department, ten thousand dollars.
Fire Marshal, five thousand dollars.
Assistant Fire Marshal, five thousand dollars.
Secretary Board of Fire Commissioners, five thousand dollars.
Storekeeper of Fire Department Yard, ten thousand dollars.

SEC. 3. City and County Officers shall not be accepted as surety for each other on official bonds. Every bond shall contain a condition that the principal will faithfully perform all official duties then, or that may thereafter be, imposed upon or required of him by law, ordinance or this Charter, and that at the expiration of his office he will surrender to his successor all property, books, papers and documents that may come into his possession as such Officer, and must also be executed by two or more sureties who shall each justify in the amount required for said bond; but when the amount of the bond is more than five thousand dollars the sureties may become severally liable for portions of not less than twenty-five hundred dollars; when there are more than two sureties said sureties may justify in an amount which, in the aggregate, shall equal double the amount of said bond.

SEC. 4. Every surety upon an official bond must make an affidavit which shall be indorsed upon such bond that he is a resident and freeholder in the City and County of San Francisco, and worth in property situated in said city and county, exclusive of incumbrances thereon, double the amount of his undertaking over and above all sums for which he is already liable or in any manner bound, whether as principal, indorser or surety, and whether such prior obligation or liability be conditional or absolute, liquidated or unliquidated, due or to become due. All persons offered as sureties on official bonds may be examined on oath as to their qualifications by the officers whose duty it is to approve the bond.

SEC. 5. When, under any of the provisions of this Charter, or of any ordinance, an official bond shall be required from an Officer, the Board of Supervisors may, by resolution, require an additional bond, whenever, in the opinion of such Board, such bond or any surety thereto, becomes insufficient; and such additional bond shall also be required when a surety to a bond shall die or cease to be a resident of said city and county.

SEC. 6. Every officer shall be liable on his official bond for the acts and omissions of the deputies, assistants, clerks and employees appointed by him, and of any and each of them, and every official bond shall contain such a condition.

SEC. 7. Every Board, Department or Officer, may require of their deputies, clerks or employees bonds of indemnity with sufficient sureties, for the faithful performance of their duties.

CHAPTER II.

OF SALARIES.

The officers hereinafter named shall respectively receive the following annual salaries, viz.:

Mayor, six thousand dollars.

Secretary of the Mayor, three thousand dollars.

Supervisors, twelve hundred dollars, each.

Clerk of Board of Supervisors, thirty-six hundred dollars.

Auditor, four thousand dollars.

Deputy Auditor, three thousand dollars.

Treasurer, four thousand dollars.

Deputy Treasurer, three thousand dollars.

Tax Collector, four thousand dollars.

Deputy Tax Collector, twenty-four hundred dollars.

Assessor, four thousand dollars.

Chief Deputy Assessor, twenty-four hundred dollars.

Recorder, thirty-six hundred dollars.

Chief Deputy Recorder, twenty-four hundred dollars.

County Clerk, four thousand dollars.

Chief Deputy County Clerk, twenty-four hundred dollars.

Sheriff, six thousand dollars.

Under Sheriff, twenty-four hundred dollars.

City Attorney, five thousand dollars.

Assistant City Attorney, thirty-six hundred dollars.

District Attorney, five thousand dollars.

Three Assistant District Attorneys, three thousand dollars, each.

Other Assistant District Attorneys, twenty-four hundred dollars, each.

Presiding Justice of the Peace, twenty-seven hundred dollars.

Four Justices of the Peace, twenty-four hundred dollars, each.

Police Judges, thirty-six hundred dollars, each.

Public Administrator, four thousand dollars.

Coroner, three thousand dollars.

Commissioners of Board of Public Works, four thousand dollars, each.

Secretary of Board of Public Works, two thousand dollars.

City Engineer, five thousand dollars.

Architect to Board of Public Works, three thousand dollars.

Superintendent of Public Works, three thousand dollars.

Storekeeper for Corporation Store Yard, twelve hundred dollars.

Superintendent of Schools, four thousand dollars.

Deputy Superintendents of Schools, three thousand dollars.

Secretary of Board of Education, twenty-four hundred dollars.

Interpreters, twelve hundred dollars.

Librarian of Public Library and Reading Rooms, twenty-four hundred dollars.

Secretary of Board of Trustees of Public Library and Reading Rooms, eighteen hundred dollars.

Three Police Commissioners, twelve hundred dollars, each.

Chief of Police, four thousand dollars.

Assistant Chief of Police, three thousand dollars.

Clerk of Chief of Police (including his pay as police officer), twenty-four hundred dollars.

Property Clerk of Police Department (including his pay as police officer), eighteen hundred dollars.

Captains of Police, twenty-four hundred dollars, each.

Sergeants of Police, fifteen hundred dollars, each.

Corporals of Police, thirteen hundred and eighty dollars, each.

Inspectors of the Police Force, fifteen hundred dollars, each.

Policemen, twelve hundred and twenty-four dollars, each.

Chief Engineer of the Fire Department, four thousand two hundred dollars.

First Assistant Engineer, three thousand dollars.

Second Assistant Engineer, twenty-four hundred dollars.

Battalion Chiefs, twenty-one hundred dollars.

Secretary Fire Department, twenty-four hundred dollars.

Assistant Secretary Fire Department, sixteen hundred and fifty dollars.

Clerk Fire Department, ten hundred and eighty dollars.

Chief of Bureau for Construction, Combustibles and Explosives, twenty-four hundred dollars.

Superintendent of Police and Fire Alarm Telegraph, twenty-seven hundred dollars.

Captains of Companies, fourteen hundred and forty dollars, each.

Lieutenants of Companies, twelve hundred dollars, each.

Engineers of Fire Engines, thirteen hundred and fifty dollars, each.

Drivers, one thousand and eighty dollars, each.

Stokers, first year, nine hundred and sixty dollars, each.

Stokers, second year, one thousand and eighty dollars, each.

Stokers, third year, twelve hundred dollars, each.

Steward, nine hundred and sixty dollars.

Hosemen and Truckmen, first class, twelve hundred dollars, each.

Hosemen and Truckmen, second class, ten hundred and eighty dollars, each.

Hosemen and Truckmen, third class, nine hundred and sixty dollars, each.

Pilots of Fireboats, twelve hundred dollars, each.

Firemen of Fireboats, nine hundred and sixty dollars, each.

Engineer of Fireboats, twelve hundred dollars, each.

Assistant Engineer of Fireboats, ten hundred and eighty dollars, each.

Clerk of Supply Department, fifteen hundred dollars.

Superintendent of Fire Engines, twenty-one hundred dollars.

Assistant Superintendent of Fire Engines, eighteen hundred dollars.

Foreman Machinist, fifteen hundred dollars.

Hydrantmen, ten hundred and eighty dollars, each.

Draymen, nine hundred dollars, each.

Watchmen, nine hundred dollars, each.

Veterinary Surgeon, seven hundred and twenty dollars.

Chief Operator Fire Alarm and Police Telegraph, eighteen hundred dollars.

Department Carpenter, thirteen hundred and fifty dollars.

Operators Fire Alarm and Police, fifteen hundred dollars, each.

Fireman of Construction Fire Alarm and Police Telegraph, twelve hundred dollars.

Assistant Fireman of Construction Fire Alarm and Police Telegraph, ten hundred and eighty dollars.

Repairers Fire Alarm and Police Telegraph, ten hundred and eighty dollars, each.

Inspector Fire Alarm and Police Telegraph, fifteen hundred dollars.

Linemen Fire Alarm and Police Telegraph, ten hundred and eighty dollars, each.

Batterymen Fire Alarm and Police Telegraph, ten hundred and eighty dollars, each.

Health Officer, three thousand dollars.

City Physician and Bacteriologist, eighteen hundred dollars.

First Assistant City Physician (Police Surgeon) fifteen hundred dollars.

Assistant Police Surgeons, twelve hundred dollars, each.

Superintendent City and County Hospital, twenty-four hundred dollars.

Assistant Superintendent City and County Hospital, fifteen hundred dollars.

Superintendent Almshouse, twenty-four hundred dollars.

Resident Physician Almshouse, fifteen hundred dollars.

Quarantine Officer, eighteen hundred dollars.

Captain of Quarantine, twelve hundred dollars.

Engineer of Quarantine, nine hundred dollars.

Superintendent City Cemetery, nine hundred dollars.

Secretary Board of Health, eighteen hundred dollars.

Health Inspectors, twelve hundred dollars, each.

Plumbing Inspector, fifteen hundred dollars.

Market Inspectors, twelve hundred dollars, each.

Assistant Market Inspectors, nine hundred dollars, each.

Election Commissioners, six hundred dollars, each.

Registrar of Voters, three thousand dollars.

Civil Service Commissioners, one thousand dollars, each.

Secretary to Civil Service Commissioners, eighteen hundred dollars.

Sec. 2. Until the Supervisors shall, by ordinance, establish the salaries and wages of the deputies, clerks and employees in the service of the city and county in the various Offices and Departments thereof which are not fixed by this Charter, the heads of the several Offices and Departments are authorized to fix the salaries and wages of such deputies, clerks and employees as they may be authorized to appoint or employ; *provided,* they shall not fix, or authorize the payment of any salary or wages at a rate higher than was the salary or wages authorized to be paid to those holding similar positions at the time this Charter takes effect.

ARTICLE XIV.

Miscellaneous.

SECTION 1. Every officer shall hold his office until the expiration of the term for which he was elected or appointed and until his successor is elected or appointed and qualified; and where no other period is prescribed, the term of such officer shall not exceed four years. An officer shall be deemed to have been "qualified" when he has taken the oath of office and filed the same, together with his official bond, if a bond is required, as herein provided.

SEC. 2. All officers, deputies, clerks, assistants and other employees of the city and county, and of the several Departments thereof, must be citizens of the United States, and during their respective terms of office or employment, must, with the exception of teachers in the Public Schools and employees in the Public Library, reside in said city and county, and have been residents of said city and county one year next preceding their appointment. They and each of them shall perform such duties as may be required of them respectively by law, ordinance, or this Charter, and shall only receive such compensation as may have been previously provided, and such compensation shall not be increased during the term of their respective offices or employment.

SEC. 3. Any person holding a salaried office under said city and county, whether by election or appointment, who shall, during his term of office, hold or retain any other civil office of honor, trust or employment under the government of the United States, or of this State (except the office of Notary Public, or officer of the National Guard), or who shall hold any other office connected with the government of said city and county, or who shall become a member of the Legislature, shall be deemed to have thereby vacated the office held by him under the city and county government.

SEC. 5. No member of the Board of Supervisors, and no officer or employee of said city and county, shall be or become, directly or indirectly, interested in, or in the performance of, any contract, work or business, or in the sale of any article, the expense, price or consideration of which is payable from the city and county Treasury; or in the purchase or lease of any real estate or other property belonging to, or taken by, said city and county, or which shall be sold for taxes or assessments, or by virtue of legal process at the suit of said city and county. If any person in this section designated shall, during the time for which he was elected or appointed, acquire an interest in any contract with, or work done for, said city and county, or any Department or officer thereof, or in any franchise, right or privilege granted by said city and county, unless the same shall be devolved upon him by law, he shall forfeit his office, and be forever after debarred and disqualified from being elected, appointed or employed in the service of said city and county; and all such contracts shall be void, and shall not be enforceable against said city and county.

Sec. 5. No officer or employee of said city and county shall give, or promise to give, to any other person, any portion of his compensation, or any money, or valuable thing, in consideration of having been, or of being, nominated, appointed, voted for, or elected to, any office or employment; and if any such promise or gift be made, the person making such gift or promise shall forfeit his office and employment, and be forever debarred and disqualified from being elected, appointed or employed in the service of said city and county.

Sec. 6. Any officer of said city and county who shall, while in office, accept any donation or gratuity in money, or other valuable thing, either directly or indirectly, from any subordinate or employee, or from any candidate or applicant for any position as employee or subordinate under him, shall forfeit his office, and be forever debarred and disqualified from holding any position in the service of said city and county.

Sec. 7. An office becomes vacant when the incumbent thereof dies, resigns, is adjudged insane, convicted of felony, or of an offense involving a violation of his official duties, or is removed from office, or ceases to be a resident of said city and county, or neglects to qualify within the time prescribed by law, or within twenty days after his election or appointment, or shall have been absent from the State without leave for more than sixty consecutive days. The Supervisors must not grant leave of absence to any officer, except for the purpose of attending to official business.

Sec. 8. Every officer authorized by law or ordinance to allow, audit or certify demands upon the Treasury,

or to make any official investigation, shall have power
to administer oaths and affirmations and take and hear
testimony concerning any matter or thing relating
thereto.

SEC. 9.   Every officer who shall approve, allow or pay
any demand on the Treasury not authorized by law, ordinance or this Charter, shall be liable to the city and
county individually, and on his official bond, for the
amount of the demand so illegally approved, allowed or
paid.

SEC. 10.   All books and records of every Office and
Department shall be open to the inspection of any citizen at any time during business hours, subject to proper
rules and regulations for the efficient conduct of the
business of such department or office.   Copies or extracts from said books and records, duly certified, shall
be given by the Officer having the same in custody, to
any person demanding the same, and paying or tender-
ing eight cents per folio of one hundred words for such
copies or extracts, and the additional sum of fifty cents
for certifying to such certified copy or extract.

SEC. 11.   Except where otherwise provided for by
law, or this Charter, all public offices shall be kept open
for business every day, except legal holidays, from half-
past eight o'clock in the forenoon until five o'clock in
the afternoon; and, in addition thereto, from the first
day of November until the last Monday of December
in each year the Office of the Tax Collector may be
kept until nine o'clock in the evening.

SEC. 12.   No person shall be eligible to, or hold, any
office, or be clerk or deputy in any Office or Department,
who, at the time of his election or appointment has not
arrived at majority, and is not a citizen of this State,
and a resident of said city and county; or who has been
found guilty of malfeasance in office, bribery, or other
infamous crime; or who in any capacity has embezzled
public funds.

SEC. 13.   The several Boards, Officers and other heads
of Departments shall annually, on or before the first
Monday in May, furnish to the Supervisors, and also to
the Auditor, a detailed estimate of the amount of money
that will be required for the expenditures of their respective Departments during the ensuing fiscal year; and on
or before the first day of August in each year, report to
the Supervisors the condition of their respective Offices

and Departments during the preceding fiscal year, embracing all their operations, receipts and expenditures. Immediately thereafter the Supervisors shall prepare and publish an abstract from said reports, and other sources, of the operations, receipts and expenditures, and condition of all Offices and Departments.

SEC. 14. All moneys, assessments and taxes belonging to, or collected for the use of the city and county, coming into the hands of any Officer of said city and county, shall immediately be deposited with the Treasurer for the benefit of the Funds to which they respectively belong. If such Officer for twenty-four hours after receiving the same shall delay or neglect to make such deposit, he shall be deemed guilty of misconduct in office and may be removed.

SEC. 15. When any Officer, Board or Department provided for in this Charter shall require additional deputies, clerks or employees, application shall be made to the Mayor therefor, and upon such application it shall be the duty of the Mayor to make investigation as to the necessity for such additional assistance; and if he find the same necessary he may recommend to the Supervisors to authorize the appointment of such additional deputies, clerks or employees; and thereupon the Supervisors, by an affirmative vote of not less than nine members, may authorize such appointments, and provide for the compensation of such appointees, subject to the limitations contained in this Charter.

SEC. 16. When the Supervisors shall determine that the public interest requires the construction or acquisition of any permanent municipal building, work, property or improvement, the cost of which in addition to the other expenditures of said city and county will exceed the income and revenue provided for said city and county, in any one year, they may, by ordinance, passed by the affirmative vote of not less than nine members of the Board, submit a proposition to incur a debt for such purpose, to the qualified electors of said city and county at a special election, to be held for that purpose only; such proposition shall specify the amount of the proposed indebtedness, the rate of interest and the specific purpose for which it is to be incurred. Such election shall be called and conducted in the same manner and under the same regulations as other elections. Should such proposition be assented to by two-thirds of the qualified electors voting at such election, the Supervisors may incur such indebtedness by issuing the bonds of said city and county to an amount not to exceed the sum named in said proposition; and before the time of incurring such indebtedness, must make provision for the collection of an annual tax sufficient to pay the interest on such indebtedness as it falls due, and also to constitute a Sinking Fund for the payment of the principal thereof within forty years from the time of contracting the same. Such bonds shall not bear over four per centum interest per annum, and must be payable in not more than forty years and shall not be sold for less than par. Said bonds must be under the seal of the city and county and signed by the Mayor, Auditor and Treasurer, and after having been so signed and sealed must be delivered to the Treasurer to be held by him in the Treasury until disposed of. All such bonds shall be sold by the Mayor, Auditor and Treasurer, for cash, to the highest bidder, after advertising for sealed proposals therefor in accordance with such regulations as may be provided in the ordinance authorizing the issue of said bonds. The money so raised shall be paid into the Treasury and there kept as a special fund, to be drawn and used only for the special purpose for which the indebtedness was incurred.

SEC. 17. No privilege shall be granted that suspends or violates any ordinance, except by an ordinance passed by the affirmative vote of not less than nine members of the Board of Supervisors.

SEC. 18. Any elected officer, except Supervisors, may be suspended by the Mayor and removed by the Board of Supervisors for cause. On the question of removal, the cause, and the ayes and noes shall be entered on the records of the Board of Supervisors. In the event of any such removal, the vacancy thus created shall be filled as provided in this Charter.

In all cases where any appointed officer shall be removed by the Mayor under the provisions of this Charter, the Mayor shall appoint some person to succeed the officer thus removed.

SEC. 19. When the Mayor shall suspend any elected officer, he shall immediately notify the Board of Supervisors of such suspension and the cause therefor. If the Board of Supervisors is not in session, he shall immediately call a session of the same in such manner as shall be provided by ordinance. The Mayor shall present written charges against such suspended officer to the Board, and furnish a copy of the same to said officer, who shall have the right to appear with counsel before the Board in his defense. If by an affirmative vote of not less than nine Supervisors, taken by ayes and noes and entered on its record, the action of the Mayor is approved, then the suspended officer shall thereby be removed from office; but if the action of the Mayor is not so approved, such suspended officer shall be immediately reinstated.

SEC. 20. When the Mayor shall remove an appointed officer from office for cause, he shall immediately notify the Board of Supervisors of such removal, and furnish it a statement of the cause thereof, which statement shall be entered in the record of its proceedings. If the Mayor fail or refuse for thirty days to make a new appointment, then the Board of Supervisors may elect a suitable person to fill the office for the unexpired term.

SEC. 21. Unless otherwise provided by law or this Charter, any Officer, Board or Department authorized to appoint any deputy, clerk, assistant or employee shall have the right to remove any person so appointed.

SEC. 22. All appointments of officers, deputies and clerks to be made under any provision of this Charter must be made in writing and in triplicate, authenticated by the person or persons, Board or Officer making the same. One of said triplicates must be filed with the Clerk of the Supervisors, another with the Auditor, and the third with the Civil Service Commission.

SEC. 23. Wherever it is provided in this Charter that the members of any Board, Department or Commission shall so classify themselves by lot that their terms of office shall expire at different times, such members shall, on the day of making such classification, cause the same to be entered in the records of their proceedings, and a copy thereof, certified by the Secretary thereof and signed by all of said members, shall be filed with the Clerk of the Supervisors.

SEC. 24. All franchises and privileges heretofore granted by said city and county, which are not in actual nse or enjoyment, or which the grantees thereof have

14

not in good faith commenced to exercise, are hereby declared forfeited and of no validity unless said grantees or their assigns shall within one year after this Charter takes effect, in good faith commence the exercise and enjoyment of such privilege or franchise.

SEC. 25. All ordinances or resolutions for the improvement of any street, for which no contract shall have been entered into at the time this Charter goes into effect, are hereby repealed.

SEC. 26. Every office, except those which are by this Charter made elective, shall become vacant immediately on the taking effect of this Charter; and the Mayor shall thereupon forthwith make the appointments provided by this Charter to be made by him. Every officer holding an office which is, by this Charter made elective, who is in office at the time this Charter shall take effect, shall hold his office until the expiration of the term for which he was elected to said office; but this shall not apply to the office of the Superintendent of Public Streets, Highways and Squares, nor to the office of City and County Surveyor, but said offices shall be abolished on the taking effect of this Charter.

SEC. 27. All officers, Boards and Commissioners shall each turn over and deliver to their respective successors designated in this Charter of the City and County of San Francisco, all papers, books, documents, records and archives in their possession or under their control respectively, or belonging to their respective offices or departments; and the respective officers or Boards to whom the same shall be delivered, must give therefor duplicate certificates, one of which shall be immediately filed in the office of the Auditor.

SEC. 28. Until the Supervisors shall by ordinance establish the number of deputies, clerks and employees to be employed in the service of the city and county in the various offices and departments thereof, the said officers and departments, respectively, may appoint and employ the same number of deputies, clerks, assistants and employees as authorized to be employed in the service of said city and county at the time this Charter takes effect.

SEC. 29. All ordinances, orders and resolutions of the City and County of San Francisco in force at the time this Charter takes effect, and not inconsistent therewith, shall continue in force until amended or repealed.

SEC. 30. Whenever at any time the Constitution and laws of the State of California shall have been so altered and amended as to permit the appointment, in lieu of the election, in the City and County of San Francisco of the Justices of the Peace, Judges of the Police Court, Board of Education, County Clerk, County Recorder, Tax Collector, Public Administrator and Coroner, it is hereby declared to be the duty of the Mayor to appoint and he shall thereafter appoint the said Justices, Judges, Board of Education and other officers and each of them to hold office for the following terms, respectively, to wit: the Justices of the Peace, Judges of the Police Court and the Board of Education for the term of four years, and the County Clerk, County Recorder, Tax Collector, Public Administrator and Coroner each for the term of two years. In case the Constitution and laws shall be so altered and amended as aforesaid before this Charter shall go into effect, then the said Justices, Judges and officers, and each of them, shall be appointed by the Mayor at the time the city and county shall be reorganized under this Charter for the terms aforesaid.

SCHEDULE.

SECTION 1. This Charter shall be published for twenty days in the "San Francisco Chronicle" and in the "Evening Bulletin," two daily papers of general circulation in the City and County of San Francisco, and after such publication, viz.: on Tuesday, the sixteenth day of April, A. D. 1895, it shall be submitted to the qualified electors of said City and County of San Francisco, at a special election which shall be held on that day, for the purpose of voting upon the adoption of the same; *provided,* that if for any reason a special election can 'not be held at said time, then this Charter shall be submitted to the qualified electors of said City and County of San Francisco at the next general election to be held in the month of November, 1896; and if a majority of the qualified electors of said city and county voting at said election shall ratify the same it shall be submitted to the Legislature of the State of California for its approval or rejection. If the Legislature shall approve the same, it shall take effect and be in force on and after the first Monday after the first day of January, A. D. 1899; *provided,* that if such approval be made prior to the first day of April, A. D. 1897, it shall take effect and be in force on and after the first Monday after the first day of July, A. D. 1897, and shall thereupon become the Charter and organic law of the City and County of San Francisco, and shall supersede the existing Charter of said city and county, and all amendments thereof, and all special laws inconsistent with this Charter.

The form of ballots at said election shall be:
"For the New Charter,"
OR
"Against the New Charter."

For the sole purpose of the election of the Officers directed in this Charter to be elected by the people, the said Charter shall take effect immediately after its approval by the Legislature, and the election of such officers shall be managed, conducted and controlled by the Board of Election Commissioners in and for said city and county in office at the time of such election, and shall be in all respects conducted in accordance with the then existing laws in relation to elections in said city and county.

At the first election to be held for municipal officers provided under this charter, and at each succeeding general election, all officers designated by this Charter shall be chosen at the election preceding the expiration of the term of office of the present incumbents of those offices.

BE IT KNOWN, That the City and County of San Francisco, containing a population of more than two hundred thousand inhabitants, on the sixth day of November, A. D. 1894, at a general election, and under and in accordance with the provisions of Section 8, Article XI, of the Constitution of this State, did elect the undersigned a Board of Freeholders, to prepare and propose a Charter for said city and county; and we, the members of said Board, in pursuance of such provisions of the Constitution, and within a period of ninety days after such election, have prepared and do propose the foregoing, signed in duplicate, as and for the Charter for said City and County of San Francisco.

IN WITNESS WHEREOF, we have hereunto set our hands in duplicate, this fourth day of February, in the year one thousand eight hundred and ninety-five.

JOSEPH BRITTON,

IRVING M. SCOTT,

M. H. HECHT,

I. J. TRUMAN,

COLIN M. BOYD,

WILLIAM F. GIBSON,

G. H. UMBSEN,

GEO. T. MARYE, JR.,

LOUIS SLOSS, JR.,

J. J. O'BRIEN,

JEROME A. ANDERSON,

HENRY N. CLEMENT.

INDEX.

247